Preaching Through the Bible

1 Corinthians 10–16

Michael Eaton

Sovereign World

Sovereign World
PO Box 777
Tonbridge
Kent, TN11 0ZS
England

By the same author:
Genesis 1–11 (Preaching Through the Bible) – Sovereign World
Genesis 12–23 (Preaching Through the Bible) – Sovereign World
Genesis 24–50 (Preaching Through the Bible) – Sovereign World
Applying God's Law (Exodus 19–24) – Paternoster
Joshua (Preaching Through the Bible) – Sovereign World
1 Samuel (Preaching Through the Bible) – Sovereign World
2 Samuel (Preaching Through the Bible) – Sovereign World
1 Kings (Preaching Through the Bible) – Sovereign World
Ecclesiastes (Tyndale Commentary) – IVP
Hosea (Focus on the Bible) – Christian Focus
Joel and Amos (Preaching Through the Bible) – Sovereign World
The Way That Leads to Life (Matthew 5–7) – Christian Focus
Mark (Preaching Through the Bible) – Sovereign World
Luke 1–11 (Preaching Through the Bible) – Sovereign World
Return to Glory (Romans 3:22– 5:21) – Paternoster
Living Under Grace (Romans 6–7) – Paternoster
1 Corinthians 1–9 (Preaching Through the Bible) – Sovereign World
1, 2 Thessalonians (Preaching Through the Bible) – Sovereign World
2 Timothy (Preaching Through the Bible) – Sovereign World
1 Peter (Preaching Through the Bible) – Sovereign World
1, 2, 3 John (Focus on the Bible) – Christian Focus
Living A Godly Life (Theology for Beginners) – Paternoster
Enjoying God's Worldwide Church (Theology for Beginners) – Paternoster
No Condemnation – IVCP (USA)
Experiencing God (Theology for Beginners) – Paternoster

ISBN: 1-85240-290-3

Typeset by CRB Associates, Reepham, Norfolk
Printed in England by Clays Ltd, St Ives plc.

Preface

There is a need for a series of biblical expositions which are especially appropriate for English-speaking preachers in the Third World. Such expositions need to be laid out in such a way that they will be useful to those who put their material to others in clear points. They need to avoid difficult vocabulary and advanced grammatical structures. They need to avoid European or North American illustrations. *Preaching Through the Bible* seeks to meet such a need. Although intended for an international audience I have no doubt that their simplicity will be of interest to many first-language speakers of English as well.

These expositions are based on the Hebrew and Greek texts but will take into account three translations of the Bible, the New King James (or Revised Authorized) Version, the New American Standard Version and the New International Version. The reader can use any of these versions alongside the exposition, and no doubt some others as well. In this exposition I have supplied my own translation.

It is not our purpose to deal with minute exegetical detail, although the commentator often has to do work of this nature as part of his preliminary preparation. But just as a good housewife likes to serve a good meal rather than display her pots and pans, so the good expositor is concerned with the 'good meal' of Scripture rather than the 'pots and pans' of dictionaries, disputed interpretations and the like. But there are lots of 'pots and pans' behind the scene. The 'chiasmus' on page 99, for example, was brought to my attention by an article on 1 Corinthians 15:20–28, by C.E. Hill, in the journal

Novum Testamentum, volume 30 (1988). Only occasionally will such matters have to be discussed, but they are there in the background. Similarly matters of 'Introduction' do not receive detailed discussion. A simple outline of some introductory matters is found in the first chapter and an appendix makes some suggestions for further study.

Michael A. Eaton

Contents

Contents

Author's Preface

These chapters continue my previous book on 1 Corinthians, which covered chapters 1–9. As always, they are the side-effect of my preaching. I preached through 1 Corinthians in Nairobi Baptist Church in the early 1980s, although I did not cover every part of it. Other parts of 1 Corinthians and of 2 Corinthians were preached in Rouxville Baptist Church in Johannesburg. Then I included a hurried survey of 1 Corinthians in the Discipleship School of Chrisco Fellowship, Nairobi, some years ago.

As always, I am grateful to the Chrisco Fellowship of Churches, in Kenya, and to Chrisco Central Church, in Nairobi, where I live for nine months of the year and which is the place I call 'home'. I am thankful to God for the different kinds of help I receive from family and friends in Nairobi. I owe a special 'thank you' to Jane Wangechi of Chrisco Central Church, and to Tim Pettingale and Chris Mungeam of Sovereign World publishers.

Michael A. Eaton

Chapter 1

The Best and the Worst

(1 Corinthians 10:1–5)

The church at Corinth seems to have been the best church and the worst church to be found in the pages of the New Testament. In some ways it was a strong and energetic church. Paul gives thanks to God that it was not lacking in any spiritual gift (1 Corinthians 1:7). It had gifts of speech and gifts of knowledge (1:5). It certainly was a lively church. No one would ever have become bored in the congregation at Corinth. It was so lively sometimes you might think they were all mad (14:23)!

1. **Most churches are a mixture of weaknesses and strengths**. We see this in the churches of the Book of Revelation (chapters 2 and 3) and we see it in the church of Corinth. Although in some ways it was the best church in New Testament times, it seems also to have been the worst of the New Testament churches. They were proud of their Greek wisdom, which was so popular in Corinth. They were choosy and critical of their preachers. There were problems of immorality. Some of the Christians were doubting the possibility of the resurrection of the dead. They were quarrelling over the gifts of the Spirit. Added to the internal confusion within the congregation, there was some distressing circumstances putting pressure on them from the outside (as 7:26 lets us know).

In 1 Corinthians 10:1 Paul is about two-thirds through a section in which he has been giving them some guidance about the 'idols-meats'. When a Christian woman in Corinth bought some meat, it had previously been offered to an idol in a pagan temple. This led to problems of conscience. Should

11

a Christian eat meat that had been used in this way? Also many social gatherings took place at the local pagan temples, but they were full of idolatry and immorality. Another difficulty for Paul was that some Corinthians were attacking him. He was willing to leave aside certain foods when eating with Jews. At other times he seemed very liberated. In order to maintain his freedom he would not accept financial support from the Corinthians.

So there are many matters that Paul must say something about. Paul puts love above knowledge. They may eat idol-meats but not at the temple! Yet they must be loving towards those with weak consciences. He warns them against being proud of their knowledge and explains his own practice. Paul lives in different ways according to where he is.

Now he warns them against getting involved in idolatry. There are not many rules and regulations in the Christian life, but we must be careful not to misuse our freedom and bring damage upon ourselves. Paul warns against idolatry and immorality especially.

2. **There is no magical protection coming from baptism or the Lord's Supper**. Paul says, *'For, brothers and sisters, I do not wish you to be ignorant of the fact that our fathers were all under the cloud and all went through the sea . . . '* (10:1). The key word is 'all'. Paul has just said that in a race all of the runners take part, but one person receives the prize. Our coming to faith is like being an athlete in a race. Our first salvation qualifies us for prize-winning. We are 'in the race' as soon as we come to salvation, but pleasing God is not automatic.

It seems that the Corinthians specially valued the symbols of baptism and the Lord's Supper. In all of Paul's letters only 1 Corinthians mentions the Lord's Supper, and 1 Corinthians 1:13–16 is perhaps Paul's only direct mention of water-baptism.[1] Clearly baptism and the Lord's Supper were specially valued – but misused – by the Corinthians. They felt that these two signs and symbols gave them some kind of protection. 'We have been baptized with water,' they said. 'That keeps us safe, even when we go to the pagan temple. And the Lord's Supper is our spiritual food that protects us.' But, Paul says, signs and symbols do not protect us when we walk into sin! The believers of ancient Israel had a kind of 'baptism', but thousands of them were punished for their sins. They 'went through the sea (10:1), and were all baptized into Moses in the cloud and in the sea ... ' (10:2). They walked through on dry land but the water was all around them. Water-baptism is an expression of faith in Christ. The first generation of Israelites consisted of a generation of believers (in fact Hebrews 11:29 treats the entire nation as great heroes of faith). Just as a modern believer **expresses** his faith by being water-baptized, so the Israelites **expressed** their faith (weak and wobbly though it was) by following Moses down into the Red Sea. It was a visible sign that they were committed to Moses and his people, just as water-baptism is a visible sign to people around us that we are committed to the Lord Jesus Christ. Israel had its own form of 'baptism', similar to the water-baptism of Christians.

Neither the fact of our being 'saved' nor our participation in baptism and the Lord's Supper abolishes the need to 'run the race' to get to our heavenly reward. Many run the race; few get the prize. The first generation of Israelites were saved by their faith in the blood of the lamb, but their failure to run the race meant that they lost their heavenly reward. It was not loss of salvation. Even Moses was among them and Moses is certainly in heaven. But it was loss of the heavenly reward because despite their great privileges they did not persist sufficiently in obedient faith towards God.

Note

[1] A few times when the word 'baptism' is used, the reference is to the Spirit rather than to water (Romans 6:3, 4; Galatians 3:27; Ephesians 4:5; Colossians 2:12). There is also 1 Corinthians 15:29 but that certainly is not a verse from which we can learn much about water-baptism.

Chapter 2

Illustrations from the Old Testament
(1 Corinthians 10:3–10)

There is (as we were seeing) no magical protection to be gained from baptism or the Lord's Supper. The Israelites had a 'baptism into Moses'. The Israelites' following Moses down into the waters of the Red Sea (although the water was around them and they did not get wet!) was very similar to the Christian's expressing his faith in Jesus.

Similarly they had something which was like the Lord's Supper. They were all baptized into Moses (10:3) *'and all drank the same spiritual drink. For they drank from the spiritual rock which followed them, and that rock was Christ'* (10:4). The first generation of Israelites had miraculously been given manna (Exodus 16:14–30) and miraculously provided with water (Exodus 17:1–7; Numbers 20:2–13). Obviously the food was physical and literal but Paul calls it 'spiritual food'. As well as providing for them physically there were also spiritual lessons in what was being given to them. The Holy Spirit had lessons to teach them as well as food and drink to feed them. Just as the Lord's Supper points to the way in which Jesus is 'bread' to us to give us spiritual life as we live on Him, so in the same way the manna that fell from heaven also pointed to God's provision of 'bread' for us in every way. God feeds our bodies; He also feeds and strengthens the life that He gives us through the Holy Spirit. Even in Old Testament times the manna from heaven was a symbol of the provision of God for every aspect of life. More than that: the bread points to Christ as the 'bread of life'.

According to a first-century Jewish legend the rock which gave water to the Israelites in the wilderness travelled with them wherever they went. Philo (the Jewish contemporary of Jesus and Paul) could say that the bread which came from heaven was 'the food of the soul'; Paul says something similar: the food which feeds and strengthens us is Christ Himself. He says in effect, 'You know the legend of a rock that travelled with them. Well, there was a "Rock" that travelled with them – the pre-existing Son of God.'

1. **The fact that we have started the Christian race does not mean that God is automatically pleased with us; we do not automatically get the heavenly prize**. The important word, repeated five times, is the word 'all'. There is good reason to think that the first generation of Israel were 'all' believers – Hebrews 11:29 says as much. Within one generation not all in Israel were **believing**, though they **descended** from that first generation (see Romans 9:6, which makes this point). But although they were at first 'all' believers who had had rich spiritual experiences, God was not pleased with many of them. *'Nevertheless, with the majority of them God was not pleased, for they were scattered in the wilderness'* (10:5).

The Christians at Corinth must realize this. The fact that they are 'saved' does not guarantee their heavenly reward. The Israelites were people who had experienced salvation (at an Old Testament level). They were even heroes of faith in the early stages of their life. But they ruined their lives and lost a great deal because they fell into sin. It is not that they lost their salvation. They did not go back to Egypt and get 'un-redeemed'. The blood of the lamb which had taken them out of Egypt was in no way reversed. They did not lose what they had, but they lost the reward God wanted to give them. One of them was Moses, who surely went to heaven. But even he lost the reward of seeing the promised land. *'Now,'* says Paul, *'these things have become patterns for us, so that we might not be people who long after evil things as those people longed after evil things'* (10:6).

2. **Paul warns us against five sins**. There were at least five dangers confronting the Israelites. The same dangers confronted the Corinthians – and they confront us as well. (i) There was the danger of **evil desire**. Paul does not want the Corinthians to 'long after evil things'. The early Israelites

could easily be dragged into desires for all sorts of worldly things; so could the Corinthians if they got involved in the pagan worship in Corinth's temples.

Paul spells out what some of these evil desires might be. (ii) There was the danger of **idolatry**. Paul says, *'And do not become idolaters as some of those did.'* (iii) There was the danger of **sexual immorality**. Paul quotes from Exodus 32:6: *'As it is written, "The people sat down to eat and drink, and they rose up to enjoy themselves"'* (10:7). By 'enjoying themselves' the text means wild revelry accompanied by immorality. *'And let us not commit immorality as some of them did, and in one day twenty-three thousand of them died'* (10:8). It is odd that Paul says 23,000; other sources that still exist say 24,000. Obviously both figures are round numbers. Josephus says the number was 14,000. We may guess that various traditions were around, some rounding the figure off to 24,000, others rounding the figure off to 23,000.

(iv) Another danger was that of **testing God**. *'And let us not test Christ as some of them did, and they were destroyed by snakes'* (10:9). Paul is stringing together various incidents in Israel's history at this period (see Numbers 11:4–6; Exodus 32:1–20; Numbers 25:1–9 and 31:16; and now Numbers 21:4–9). 'Testing God' is sinning in the hope that He will do nothing about it. (v) A fifth danger was that of **grumbling**. *'And do not grumble as some of them did and they were destroyed by the destroying angel'* (10:10). The Corinthians were grumbling against Paul; but God hates it when we complain either against God or against His chosen servants.

Chapter 3

Enduring in Time of Temptation
(1 Corinthians 10:11–15)

Paul is warning the Corinthians against the kind of sins they might fall into if they go the pagan temples in Corinth: evil desire, idolatry, sexual immorality, testing God and grumbling. But he has some encouragements to give them also.

1. **He warns against presuming that we cannot fail**. Paul has been quoting Old Testament Scriptures. Everything that happened in the days of the Old Testament Scriptures has been recorded for the benefit of those who live in the gospel age. *'Now these things happened to them as an example, and they were written down for us as a warning for us upon whom the ends of the ages have come'* (10:11). Since the coming of Christ into the world it is an age when all things are being brought to fulfilment and completion. The biblical records of the previous epochs of history were kept in order that the final age, the age in which we live, might benefit from what has happened before. Paul expects us to read and ponder Old Testament stories and apply their lessons to ourselves.

One great lesson that we shall learn from the Old Testament is the danger of taking God's grace for granted. *'So let the person who supposes he stands watch out lest he fall'* (10:12). The story of the Israelites will teach us that those who have had great beginnings may still fall and ruin the latter days of their lives. Those who had enjoyed such rich experiences at the time of the crossing of the sea with Moses, later ruined their lives and came under God's judgement. So Paul asks us to be careful of presumption and self-confidence.

2. **He reminds them that they are no different from other people**. He says, *'No testing has come upon you, except what is*

common to other people' (10:13a). We all tend to feel that our case is special! Perhaps we feel that we have temptations or troubles that are greater than those of other people. Perhaps we feel justified in doing something that is not permitted to others. The Corinthians who went to pagan worship at the Corinth felt justified in doing so.

They said something like this: 'We realize that normally one should not go to a pagan temple, but in our case there is a good reason why we should go. We are an exceptional case. We shall be cut off from our fellow Corinthians if we do not join in this worship in the temple. We do not really believe in it but there are special, exceptional reasons why we should join in with this worship. It is idolatry for them but an idol is nothing, so we are not really indulging in any sin by going to the idolatrous worship.'

Paul says: 'No, your situation is no different from anyone else's. No testing has come upon you except what is experienced by other people as well as by yourselves. You are not exceptional. You do not have any special excuse. Everyone is tempted to compromise with sin and so are you. You must not think that you have some special reason which entitles you to do things which are forbidden to others.'

3. **He reminds them of the way in which God sets a limit to temptation**. We must keep in mind that Paul's Greek word here (*peirasmos*) means both 'tempting' and 'testing'. It could be translated 'temptation-and-testing'. Every temptation is a test; every test is a temptation. Paul writes, *'And God is faithful. He will not allow you to be tempted or tested beyond what you are able to endure, but with the testing He will provide also the outcome so that you can endure it'* (10:13b).

In the middle of any tempting or testing situation we shall discover the faithfulness of God. He will always do two things. (i) He will set a limit to the testing situation; it will not actually be beyond our ability to bear it. He will set a limit to how heavy it is; and generally He will set a limit to how long it lasts. If it is never to be taken away exceptional grace will be given (see 2 Corinthians 12:9). (ii) He has in mind an 'outcome', an 'end-result'. If we endure in any situation of testing, resisting the temptation to do anything sinful, we shall find there is both an end to the situation and (more important) an 'end-result'. God will do something wonderful to us and for us, if we do not give in to temptation and turn to sin. It is our knowledge that there will be an 'outcome' that enables us to endure in time of testing or temptation. (The word does not exactly mean 'escape'; if you 'escape' temptation then you do not have to endure it!)

All of this now leads Paul to address himself directly to the dangers of idolatry confronting the Christians in Corinth.

1. **The Christian must not get involved in idolatry**. Or – to put it in a modern way – we must not get involved in other religions. Paul says, *'Therefore, my beloved friends, flee from idolatry'* (10:14). This might shock many modern people. They like to think that all religions are more or less the same. Nowadays people tolerate anything – so long as you never say that any religion is wrong! Paul did not take that view. If the God of the Bible is the true God – and He is – then other ways of talking about God are faulty and misleading. Other so-called 'gods' are in fact idols.

2. **Paul wants us to have an understanding of what is involved in idolatry**. He says, *'I am speaking to you as wise people. You – consider for yourselves what I am saying'* (10:15). The idea is around in some places that Christians should not use their minds. Paul says the exact opposite: Consider! Think! Decide for yourself, using your own spiritual wisdom. You have the anointing of the Holy Spirit. Trust God to lead you. 'Gird up your minds' (1 Peter 1:13). As Christians we do not trust our **unaided** mind; we do not 'lean upon our own understanding' (Proverbs 3:5), but we are to be willing to think. God the Spirit will lead us as we think! We shall see that idolatry is something to be avoided.

Chapter 4

Refusing Idolatry

(1 Corinthians 10:16–22)

There are good reasons why Christians should not get involved with idolatry. If the Corinthians think a little, enlightened by the Holy Spirit, they will see how foolish it is to get involved with idols.

3. **'Religious' meals involve fellowship with the one you are worshipping**. Many of the Corinthians were saying to themselves, 'These idol-meats are nothing. We can eat them and we shall not be affected.' They were right to say that when they were thinking of meals in their own homes, but **religious** meals at the temple were a different matter. Paul is not criticizing the Corinthians for eating the idol-meats but he is criticizing them for getting involved in idolatry.

A Kenyan MP (Member of Parliament) once said to me: 'I am a Christian but many people in my constituency are Moslems. They want me to speak at a ceremony opening some welfare organization. Is it all right for me to do something like that?'

I said: 'Yes, you are their Member of Parliament. You represent them. They are your people as much as any others in your constituency. But if they ask you to take part in their prayers – you ought to ask politely to be excused from praying to their "Allah".' We can share 'neutral' meals and activities with other people, but we do not get involved in their pagan religion. We need not fear that meat – or any other material object – is contaminated with demons, but we do not get involved with the demons present in pagan **worship**.

Paul illustrates his point from the Lord's Supper. At pagan meals there would be a lot of eating and drinking in honour of the god or the gods. Many Christians were saying, 'We know that there is no such thing as any other god, so maybe it does not do any harm to join in with the pagan worship. *We* are not believing in any demon. We are just there for the food and drink with our neighbours.' Paul says: 'No, you are not right. Actually when you are involved in a **religious** meal, you are having **fellowship** with whatever god or demon is involved.'

This leads Paul to talk about the Lord's Supper in order to illustrate what goes on at pagan religious gatherings. What happens in **their** gatherings is parallel to what happens in **our** gatherings. But in **their** gatherings they are fellowshipping with demons; in **our** gatherings we are enjoying fellowship with the Lord, the God and Father of our Lord Jesus Christ.

'The cup of blessing for which we give thanks, is it not a participation in the blood of Christ? And is not the bread that we break a participation in the body of Christ?' (10:16). What is the Lord's Supper? (i) It is a means of keeping the cross of Christ central in the life of the church. There is always a danger that the church of Jesus Christ will drift away from its central message. But the central experience of the Christian church is our experience of the cross of Jesus Christ. What is the cross of Jesus Christ? It achieves many things, but it is first and foremost God's way of salvation from the death penalty that is attached to sin. The wages of sin is death – in many senses of the word. But Jesus 'died'. His blood pays the price for our sins. The Lord's Supper is primarily connected with salvation from sin. (It is not **primarily** connected with physical healing. If you use the Lord's Supper in the right way it is certain you will be forgiven. But even if you use the Lord's Supper in the right way it is not **certain** that you will be physically healed.)

What is the Lord's Supper? (ii) Among other things, it is a symbolic meal. The **wine** symbolizes the blood of Jesus Christ. The **bread** symbolizes the body of Christ upon the cross. The **breaking** symbolizes the sufferings of Christ. The **one loaf** symbolizes the unity of the fellowship. *'Because there is one loaf, we who are many are one body, for we all share in the* *one loaf'* (10:17). Paul uses the word 'body' here to refer to the church. In the previous sentence it referred to the literal body of Christ upon the cross.

What is the Lord's Supper? (iii) It is an occasion for fellowship with Jesus in the blessings of the gospel. It is a 'participation in the blood of Christ', a 'participation in the body of Christ'. On our side there is faith. We are telling God again that we believe in the blood of Christ, that we know Jesus died for us in His body (10:16).

How should the Lord's Supper be used? (i) With gratitude. We 'give thanks for' the bread and for the wine, because we are grateful for what they say to us about Jesus. (ii) With faith. We believe again in Jesus' death upon the cross. We believe again in the power of His blood to forgive our sins and minister to us peace of conscience.

'Consider the people of Israel. Do not those who eat the sacrifices participate in the altar? (10:18). *Do I mean then a sacrifice offered to an idol is anything?'* (10:19). *'No, but the sacrifices of pagans are offered to demons, not to God, and I do not want you to be participants with demons* (10:20). *You cannot drink the cup of the Lord and the cup of demons too. You cannot have a part in both the Lord's table and the demon's table* (10:21). *Are we trying to arouse the Lord's jealousy? Are we stronger than He?'* (10:22). If religious meals involve fellowship with the one with whom you are worshipping, then we ought to realize that we can go to the Lord's Supper but we cannot go to any demon's supper! If a Christian tries to do so he or she will arouse the jealousy of God.

Chapter 5

Freedom Limited by Love
(1 Corinthians 10:23–11:1)

Paul now brings this discussion to an end. The question he has been answering is: can Christians participate in idolatrous worship at the pagan temples? For the modern Christian there are similar questions: can the Christian share in pagan thinking and living? Can we be involved in the religions of the world?

1. **There are limits to freedom** (10:23–24). Paul returns to the slogans he had mentioned before. *'All things are lawful, but not all things are profitable. All things are permissible, but not all things build up'* (10:23). Paul agrees with the saying, 'All things are lawful', but he adds some limits to it. There is a sense in which it is true. God's world is to be enjoyed. Everything created by God is good. Nothing is to be rejected if it is received with gratitude (see 1 Timothy 4:4). There is no condemnation to those who are in Christ Jesus. Every sin may be forgiven.

But the Christians must not misuse their security. Paul wants the Corinthian Christians to feel free to enjoy God's world but he does not want them to press their freedom so far that they do damage to themselves. The Corinthians' desire to attend the social gatherings at the temple will not in fact help them, and it will not build up other people. We must ask ourselves questions about what is helpful. Will what I am planning help my health? My emotional state? My spiritual sensitivity? My understanding of God and His Word? Will it damage someone else? Will it damage another person's conscience? Will it affect the church's testimony? Freedom is to be restricted by love for the other person. Will what I am about to do build up the Christian fellowship? *'Let no one seek his own advantage but let him think of what is good for the other person'* (10:24).

2. **Paul comes to two conclusions**. (i) Eating 'idol-meats' is all right and need not bother us if our doing so does not affect others and is not part of pagan religion. *'Eat anything sold in the meat-market and do not ask questions on account of conscience* (10:25). *For the earth is the Lord's and so is everything that fills it'* (10:26). The material things of this world are not evil in themselves. Sinners may misuse them but that need not cause us difficulties. The world is not owned by sinners or by Satan. It is owned by God, and we may have freedom to enjoy God's world, and its contents. The meat on sale in the market may have been sacrificed to an idol but the substance of it is not changed. The Corinthian Christian may buy it and eat it, without fear of sinning. *'If anyone of the unbelieving people invites you to a meal, and you want to go, eat whatever is put before you and do not ask questions for the sake of conscience'* (10:27).

(ii) There is, however, a limit to the freedom Paul gives to the Corinthian Christians. *'But if someone says to you, "That food is something that has been offered in sacrifice", then do not eat it, for the sake of the one who informed you and also for the sake of conscience* (10:28) – *I mean not your conscience but the other person's conscience'* (10:29a). If, when a Christian is about to eat some meat, someone points out that it has been offered in sacrifice, then the Christian should ask to be excused. Who is this other person? Probably a fellow guest at the meal. Paul is very concerned to win unsaved people to Jesus. He will not cause perplexity to a person who is interested in listening to his message. If Paul is about to eat something that has been offered in sacrifice but it causes perplexity to an onlooker (who wonders whether a Christian is honouring the pagan god to whom the meat was offered) – then Paul will leave aside that meal. He does so not for God's sake or his own sake, but to avoiding confusing the pagan man watching him. The pagan man has a 'conscience' – not a desire to please God but an awareness of right and wrong. He thinks that maybe Paul is sinning by eating this meat. He does not mind sinning himself but he is surprised to find Paul doing something that he (the pagan) thinks might be sin for Paul.

In 1 Corinthians 10:29b he picks up from 10:27. *'For why is my freedom being judged by another person's conscience?* (10:29b). *If I take the meal with gratitude, why I am criticized for something in which I give thanks to God?'* (10:30). Evidently some felt Paul should not eat idol-meats ever! But when the circumstances are right and Paul is in a private home, he has freedom to eat meat of any kind he likes. The earth is the Lord's and so is everything that fills it. Christians do not need to be in bondage to other people's legalisms. Unless there is special reason why Paul should limit himself, he is free!

3. **Paul closes this section with three guidelines**. The Christian is to be concerned about (i) God's glory. *'So whether you eat or drink or whatever you do, do everything for the honour of God'* (10:31). The Christian is to be concerned about (ii) good witness. *'Do not cause anyone to stumble, whether they are Jews or Greeks or the church of God . . .'* (10:32). Christians must neither confuse unsaved people nor weak Christians.

The Christian is to follow apostolic example (11:1). Do not cause anyone to stumble, (10:32), *'just as I also seek to please all people in all things. I am not seeking my own pleasure but what helps the people, so that they may be saved* (10:33). *Be followers of me, just as I also am a follower of Christ'* (11:1).

Chapter 6

Men and Women in Corinth
(1 Corinthians 11:2–9)

In 1 Corinthians 11:2–14:40 Paul comes to a new major section in his letter. He now deals with various disorders in public worship, in connection with **men and women in worship** (11:2–16), **the Lord's Supper** (11:17–34), and **the gifts of the Holy Spirit** (12:1–14:40).

1. **First Paul commends them** (11:2). He says, *'Now I praise you because you remember me in every way, and you keep the traditions just as I handed them on to you'* (11:2). To 'hand something on' is a way of speaking about tradition. Tradition is to be resisted when it overthrows God's Word, but God's Word may *itself* be handed down as tradition. Paul's apostolic instruction could be 'handed down' as something he wanted to be received as inspired tradition in the churches. Good traditions in the New Testament included instructions about behaviour (see 2 Thessalonians 3:6) and stories about what Jesus did (see 1 Corinthians 11:23–25). Paul is speaking generally. In most matters the Corinthians followed Paul's tradition (especially in connection with the Lord's Supper) although there are some in which matters he is just about to correct them.

2. **Next he gives a basic statement about an order of authority** (11:3). There is a hierarchy of authority: God → Christ → man → woman. *'Now I want you to know that the head of every man is Christ, and the head of every woman is the man, and the head of Christ is God'* (11:3). 'Head' implies leadership, authority and provision. (The suggestion that it means 'source' cannot be maintained.) Men and women are equally children of God but this does not mean men and women are

identical in every way; the New Testament suggests otherwise. Paul is dealing with function not status. God and His Son are equally divine, but the Father sends the Son. The Father is the leader within the Godhead. In the Church man and woman are equally children of God (Galatians 3:28) but in *function* the man is the leader.

We may ask: **why was this teaching needed?** There were clearly women in Corinth who were excited by the idea of equality of the sexes in their equal **salvation** (taught by Paul in Galatians 3:28). 'The age of the Holy Spirit has come,' they said. 'Traditional structures in society can be thrown aside – now!' But they were taking this to imply that men and women are totally identical in their leadership roles. This was a mistake and Paul is correcting it. There is neither male nor female in Christ, but this does not mean that men should bear children and breast-feed them! Men and women are not identical in every way. It seems there were women in Corinth who wanted to act like men. So they arranged their hair (or head-covering) in a way that copied the Christian men. Paul says this is a mistake. Spiritual equality as God's children? Yes! Identical function in every respect? No!

3. **Positions of authority are to be culturally expressed**. There are two possible ways of translating 11:4–7. One line of interpretation thinks the passage is about a covering cloth over the head. The interpretation goes like this:

A man must not pray or prophesy with any kind of shawl. A covered head is a mark of subjection and men are the leaders of the congregation so should not wear any sign of subjection (11:4). On the other hand a woman (says this line of interpretation) should wear a head-covering as a sign of subjection to the men (11:5). If she refuses she is behaving like an immoral woman. It is like having one's head shaved (which is **also** a sign of immorality). If she is willing to be like a prostitute in one way, she should be willing to be like a prostitute in another way (11:6). A man, however, ought to have an uncovered head. This is a sign that he has the image of God in a greater way than the woman (11:7).

The question, however, is this: do verses 4–7 really speak of head-coverings or do they speak of long hair? The Greek more literally translated speaks of 'having something hanging down'. It has often been thought that this refers to some kind of veil or head-covering. Yet actually there is another possibility. 'Having something hanging down' might equally refer to having long hair hanging down. And there are good reasons for thinking this is the meaning. Consider two passages in the Greek Old Testament. First, in Numbers it says: *'Speak to the Israelites and say to them: "If a man's wife ... is unfaithful ... The priest shall ... make her stand before the Lord ... he shall **loosen her hair**"'* (Numbers 5:11–12, 16, 18), and in Leviticus *'As to the leper ... his garments shall be torn and his head shall be **with loose hair** ...'* (Leviticus 13:45). These two passages both use similar Greek wording to what we have in 1 Corinthians 11:4–7 but the reference is not to veils or head-coverings. It is to the way in which a person's hair hangs loose or is done up in a knot on top of the head or is cut short. To my mind it is far more likely (as the margin of the New International Version has it) that the reference in 1 Corinthians 11:4–7 is to the way in which a woman wears her hair. So another interpretation – and to my mind a better one – goes like this:

A man must not pray or prophesy with long hair. To do so dishonours his head (Christ). Long womanly hair is a sign of womanliness. Men are the leaders of the congregation so should not have their hair in any woman's style (11:4). On the other hand a woman (says this line of interpretation) should in public worship have her hair tied up in a knot covering the head, as a sign of subjection to the men (11:5). If she has long hair hanging down in public worship she is behaving like an immoral woman. If she acts like a man she dishonours her 'head' (husband or male leader of the family). It is like having one's head shaved (which is **also** a sign of immorality). If she is willing to be like a prostitute in one way, she should be willing to be like a prostitute in another way (11:6). A man, however, ought to have an uncovered head – that is, should be without a knot of long hair upon his head. This is a sign that he has the image of God in a greater way than the woman (11:7).

In verse 8 Paul begins to substantiate what he has said. Man has priority in creation (11:8); womankind was created to be a helpmate to the man, not the other way round (11:9). We need follow the argument no further for the moment. Three practical lessons emerge from our passage so far.

1. **It is clear that women may participate in public worship with men**. There would be no point in saying how women should behave **when** they pray or prophesy if they do not pray or prophesy at all. The teaching of 1 Corinthians 14:34–35 and 1 Timothy 2:9–15 cannot be used to overthrow this fact. Clearly women were involved in public praying and worship-leading. Attempts to deny this fact must be rejected.

2. **In general male leadership is asserted**. This, says Paul, is part of the way men and women are created.

3. **There is a difference between spiritual principles and the way they are expressed in any particular culture**. Does the modern Christian woman have to have long hair (impossible for some!) or wear a head-covering? No. We maintain the **principle** (in 11:3), but the **expression** of it may be updated. In 1 Corinthians we accept male leadership, but the way in which it has to show itself in hairstyle of head-coverings is of no relevance to the twenty-first century. There is a difference between permanent principles and those **same** principles expressed in a local and cultural way. We accept the need of humility but the command 'Wash one another's feet' may be updated. We accept the need of Christian greetings but 'Give a holy kiss' will have to be changed in many cultures. In 1 Corinthians 11:3 the teaching is principle. In 1 Corinthians 11:4–7 it is culture.

Chapter 7

God's Order in Creation
(1 Corinthians 11:10–16)

In the story of Genesis 2, man was created first and was given work to do (Genesis 2:8–17). Then the woman was created (Genesis 2:18–25) to be a helpmate for him. As Paul says (1 Corinthians 11:8–9), it was in that order, not the other way around. This order of responsibility is God's created way of doing things. Both men and women are created in the image of God, but part of that 'image of God' is dominion over creation. **Generally** men and women are **equally** in the image of God, but in the matter of **authority** the woman's authority over creation involves her being under the authority of male leadership. This is the point of 11:7; it is important to add that the biblical idea of leadership is a humble and tender one.

So, says Paul, *'For this reason the woman ought to have authority on her head because of the angels'* (11:10). The woman has authority herself when she submits to God's authority and male authority. Her visible womanliness (however it may be expressed in our culture) is a sign of **her** authority over creation which she has when she herself is under male leadership. One expects Paul to be talking about man's authority but he talks about the woman's authority! Translations which speak of 'a **sign** of (male) authority on (the woman's) head' have missed what Paul precisely says. She has **her** authority when she is shepherded by **his** authority.

'Because of the angels' probably means 'because angels are invisibly present at every worship meeting'. We worship in an orderly manner, without letting women use the occasion to assert a leadership which is not theirs – as was happening in Corinth. We maintain the kind of orderliness that the angels will approve of. Why did Paul mention this? It must have something to do with discussions and debates taking place among the Corinthians who (it seems) were specially interested in angels. Perhaps 1 Corinthians 6:3 is there for the same reason.

In **verses 11–12** Paul goes back to explain the way men and women were created. Verse 11 says: Man gave rise to woman (in Genesis 2:22). Woman gives rise to man (every time a baby is born). Verse 12 draws a deduction: men and women need each other. When men act without women things go wrong. When women act without men things go wrong. This is the arrangement that comes from God (11:12): partnership and leadership at the same time.

In verses 13–15 Paul appeals to 'nature'. It is natural to sense that men are born to be leaders. The human race is created with this instinct (which is why recent movements of thought have brought **some** changes for the good but when pressed too far it begins to feel 'unnatural'). It is also natural (Paul's precise point here) to express that feeling within the culture in which we have grown up. It Corinth it would have been 'natural' to express womanly co-operation with male leadership by appropriate hairstyle or head-covering (11:13). It would have been 'natural' for women to have long hair and men short hair (11:14–15a).

One has to say that, in a different culture from that of the first-century Mediterranean world, it is still 'natural' to feel that men should be in a leadership role. But the way in which that is visibly expressed will be 'natural' for different people in different ways. For some people women wearing trousers will be 'unnatural' and unfeminine. In other places women will wear trousers **without** seeming to be unfeminine.

The word 'uncovered' in verse 13 might mean 'without a covering-cloth' or it might mean 'without a covering knot of hair' (I prefer the latter but in the end it is not important which is in view; both were cultural expressions only).

Verse 15b affects the interpretation of the whole passage. If it means 'women have hair *instead* of a covering' it is proof that the whole passage is about hair not head-cloths! This seems to me to be the right interpretation. Others take it to mean 'women have hair **as** a covering' – which implies that in worship women have two coverings, hair plus another one! The difference of interpretation is unimportant. This aspect of the matter only concerns culture and is not obligatory in modern churches.

In verse 16 Paul appeals to the unity of all the churches. For all time (the matter is based upon creation) men are to be the leaders in the churches, in a sensitive manner, allowing much freedom and abundant opportunities for the involvement of women. Yet also for the moment (this aspect of the ruling is not everlasting) this must be **expressed** in a manner that is natural for all the churches in that first-century Mediterranean area. The wisdom of the churches is to be heeded. Corinthian women who are getting overexcited about taking over leadership must follow the wisdom of the churches as a whole. Neither Paul nor the churches will accept their ambitions to break out of the order of God's creation. In Christ they have equal status as Christians and abundant opportunities for ministry, but let women be women and men be men.

In these days of 'equality of women' we need to ask how to apply all of this. Space allows only two comments. (i) In the past, and still in areas where Christian influence is not great, women have been badly oppressed. When the gospel reaches that part of the world, the women are given greater status and liberty. 1 Corinthians 11 must not be misused; Christians should be first and foremost in the task of releasing women from being oppressed. In the churches they may do **almost** everything that the men do. (ii) But we must not go from one extreme to the other. Equality of status as people made in God's image is **not** the same as exact identity of function. On a committee there will be a chairman. The chairman is not **superior** but is a **leader** for reasons of order and to ensure the smooth-flowing of business. In the 'committee' of the human race man is not **superior** but he has been given a **leadership role**. Cultural expressions of principles may change, but obedience to Scripture's basic principles themselves must stand.

Chapter 8

Disunity in the Church of God
(1 Corinthians 11:17–22)

Paul is still dealing with disorders in public worship, as he turns now to write about the Lord's Supper (11:17–34). His first concern is the disunity of the congregation. *'Now as I give you this instruction, I am not praising you, because you are gathering together not for the better but for the worse'* (11:17). He had praised them before (11:1), but he cannot praise them at this point. He explains: *'For, in the first place, when you come together in assembly I hear that there are divisions among you, and in part I believe it'* (11:18).

1. **There may be useful and there may be sinful division in the church**. What is the **sin** of disunity? There can be a division in the church of God without it being sinful. It is not wrong to have a division in the church (i) when, in order to evangelize, part of the church moves elsewhere to start a new congregation in line with the agreed policy of the church. (ii) It is not sinful if God's people take action when part of the church ceases to be the church because of its rejection of the gospel. The apostles separated from the temple eventually when it became clear that the old people of God, Israel, had no intention of accepting Jesus as Messiah. That is not a division in the church at all. It is simply the church insisting on keeping its gospel-message clear. True believers are not a 'wing' of the church! We do not allow a false gospel. (iii) We are not sinning if some kind of division is necessary to retain the character of the church. If tradition is forcing the church to be out of its true character, if the nature of the church as a spiritual people is not being upheld, if there is interference with freedom of worship – then the Christians can take action

in these situations without it being sin. **Accusations** of divisiveness are not always justified.

But the divisiveness in Corinth was sinful. It was caused by worldliness, being obsessed with physical desires, replacing the gospel with a love of wisdom, using the gifts of the Spirit for purposes of pride, and – as we learn here in 1 Corinthians 11 – social snobbishness. When people are wanting to be superior to the poor, or they want to boast about their social status, then the **sin** of divisiveness is being committed. The sin of disunity can also be caused by bringing in rites and ceremonies into the church, and by bigotry (a blind, un-reasoning and unreasonable obsession about some minor matter of opinion).

2. **A temptation to disunity tests spiritual character**. Paul says: In part I believe it (11:18), *'For it is necessary also for there to be divisions among you in order that the people of character might become obvious among you'* (11:19). Nothing tests our spiritual character more than what shows itself at a time when we are tempted to disunity. It is at such a point that it is revealed who are people of love, and who are people that practise discrimination. The church will always face **temptations** to disunity, times when hints of disunity appear. It is at such times that a person's spiritual maturity, or lack of it, is revealed.

3. **We have to take the trouble not to allow discrimination in the church**. In Corinth the pride of the majority and their love of wisdom and social status was damaging the fellowship. *'When you gather together in one place it is not the Lord's Supper you eat* (11:20), *for each of you takes his own supper, and one person is hungry and another is drunk'* (11:21). They were forgetting that the Lord's Supper is not just a social occasion, it is something ordained by our Lord Jesus Christ. It is His supper; He is the host and He is feeding all of His people. It was wicked to be using it as a kind of party in which people ate too much and drank too much wine, and ill-treated the poorer Christians! God hates it when we discriminate against poorer people in the church. Poor people are not to be treated badly. And they are not to be treated patronizingly either! We are to realize that wealth counts for **nothing** in the

eyes of God. The rich are not rich when they come to church. The poor are not poor. We are simply ex-sinners, forgiven sinners, people wanting to know God. Poverty and wealth do not come into the matter at all!

4. **We must not forget the importance of the church**. We do not treat the congregation of God's people as unimportant or trivial. *'Do you not have houses in which to eat and drink? Or do you despise the church of God, and do you embarrass those who have nothing? What shall I say to you? Shall I praise you? In this I do not praise you!'* (11:22). The church of God is precious to Him. We do not use it as a social club or a musical society or a debating forum or a political agency – and certainly not as a party to meet our friends and be unkind to the poor! The church of Jesus Christ is the place where the redeemed have fellowship. It is the fellowship of the saved! We come together to encourage one another in the things of God, and to have Jesus feed us with the cross. The church of God is so precious to Him that if we misuse it He will be displeased. Jesus is building His Church. We are to build it with Him, not slow the progress of the building or pull it down. Those who love Jesus must love His people.

Chapter 9

The Lord's Supper
(1 Corinthians 11:23–26)

The Corinthians have been misusing the Lord's Supper and using it into a worldly party for themselves and their Christian friends, a party in which some of the poorer members of the fellowship have been badly treated. But now Paul reminds them of the original instructions of Jesus.

1. Paul speaks of **a revelation which he had received.** *'For I received from the Lord that which I also passed on to you . . .'* (11:23a). Paul received a revelation from the Lord Jesus Christ. It is sometimes asked: does this refer to a purely supernatural revelation or did some of the facts come to Paul as a tradition from the earlier apostles? We know from Paul's writings generally that the answer is: a mixture of both. The basic **interpretation** contained in his message came from his experience on the Damascus Road. Fuller details of the night before the crucifixion were no doubt given to him by earlier apostles. Both the supernatural and the more natural revelations came from 'the Lord'. Information from Peter would have been from 'the Lord' just as much as instruction from Jesus on the Damascus Road, and supernatural insight from the ascended Lord Jesus Christ. It all came 'from the Lord'.

2. Paul speaks of **the meaning of the bread.** *'I received . . . that which I also passed on to you, that the Lord Jesus on the night in which He was betrayed took bread* (11:23), *and having given thanks He broke it and said, "This is my body which is for you. Do this in remembrance of me"'* (11:24).

It was **an occasion for thanksgiving**. Jesus gave thanks for the bread.

36

The bread symbolised **the body of Jesus**. It reminds us of the fact that Jesus literally bore our sins in His body on the tree (1 Peter 2:24). Of course the bread is not **literally** the body of Jesus. The **literal** body of Jesus was standing there holding the bread in His hands. 'This is my body' means 'This represents my body' (just as, in Revelation 1:20, *'The seven lamps are the seven churches'* means 'The seven lamps represent the seven churches').

The breaking symbolised **participation**, for the bread could not be shared without being broken. The broken bread also symbolizes **suffering**. Some Greek manuscripts have 'which is broken for you' in verse 24, but they are the less reliable ones. The best manuscripts have 'which is for you'. Actually not one of Jesus' bones was broken on the cross. Yet Jesus did suffer immensely in His death upon the cross. The greatest part of His suffering was being abandoned by the Father.

The eating of the bread is an occasion for **remembrance**. We must not get too superstitious about this word. There is no repetition of the sacrifice of Christ. Jesus died once-for-ever and that sacrifice is finished and complete. Nor must we get too 'magical' in thinking about the Lord's Supper as if mysterious spiritual magic was taking place without our knowing it. The visible bread and wine stirs our faith and points our memory in the right direction. But the 'remembering' is not the remembering of a dead friend; it is remembering a living Saviour. Although Jesus is not **in** the bread and wine, He is present as we pray and as we believe. We remember what our **living** Saviour who is present with His people did for us for our redemption. It is the bread and wine that makes us thank Him for the greatest thing He ever did: His death upon the cross.

3. Paul speaks of **the meaning of the cup of wine**. *'In the same way also He took the cup, after the supper, saying "This cup is the new covenant in my blood. Do this, as often as you drink it, in remembrance of me"'* (11:25).

The cup speaks symbolically of the new covenant (22:20) – an offer of God in which He relates to us, gives us certain promises, and offers to confirm the promise by the taking of an oath. Every covenant has to involve sacrifice at one point or another. There can be no covenant without 'the blood of the covenant'. What makes it possible for us to be in relation with God is the death of Jesus for our sins. That is the 'blood of the covenant'. The wine speaks of the blood which keeps us in covenant with God and enables us to continue in obedience and faith until God swears the covenant oath and we inherit what He is wanting to give us.

4. Paul speaks of **the proclamation of Jesus' death**. *'For as often as you eat this bread and drink the cup, you proclaim the Lord's death until He comes'* (11:26). The Lord's Supper is a way of preaching to ourselves. We **listen** to preaching in the words of the preacher. We **see** the preaching when we gaze upon the bread and wine (which should let us know that our eyes should not be closed during this time!). We gather together and preach to each other in visible form as well as in spoken words, when we eat bread and drink wine in commemoration and gratitude to Jesus. We shall have to go on reminding each other of the cross of Christ in this way until He comes, and then we shall need no reminding.

So the Lord's Supper is God's way of getting us to keep the cross of Christ central in the life of the church. We use the Lord's Supper to draw close to Jesus in gratitude for what He has done for the entire Church through His cross – and as we do so Jesus draws near to us. The visible symbols of bread and wine will not be empty symbols. Because they direct our faith, they become powerful channels of blessing to us. Jesus is not specially present in bread and wine, but He comes close to us when we use the sight of bread and wine to praise Him for His cross, and take His cross into our lives more than ever.

Chapter 10

Approaching the Lord's Table
(1 Corinthians 11:27–34)

Now Paul moves on to tell us how to approach the Lord's Supper. He has reminded us of its origin. It preaches Christ's death to us until He comes. But how should we approach the Lord's table?

1. **We avoid eating the Supper in an inappropriate way** (11:27). Paul says: *'The conclusion is: whoever eats the bread or drinks the cup of the Lord in an inappropriate way is sinning against the body and blood of the Lord'* (11:27). We notice that the worshipper both ate bread and drank wine. The Roman Catholic custom of withholding the wine receives no support from Scripture.

The old 'King James' version of the Bible translated this verse 'whosoever shall eat ... unworthily'. But of course no one is 'worthy' of the Lord's Supper. What Paul has in mind is the way the Corinthians are ill-treating the poor and forgetting what it means to be church. Who can come to the Lord's Supper without feeling sinful? If we were able to live worthily in **that** sense we would not need the blood of Christ. The blood of Christ was shed for unworthy people, people needing forgiveness and cleansing. All are unworthy in that sense of the term. What Paul has in mind is the wickedness of coming to the Lord's Supper without concern for the unity of the church in the gospel. Sinning against fellow Christians is sinning against the body and blood of the Lord.

Paul refers to the actual events being remembered. There is no literal body and blood of the Lord in the bread and wine themselves. But the person who comes carelessly is forgetting the greatness of what Jesus did for us. He died in His body,

He shed His blood, in order to bring in a company of people who are one in Christ. Sinning against fellow Christians is sinning against the cross.

2. **We examine ourselves** (11:28). *'But let each person test himself, and so let each one eat of the bread and drink from the cup'* (11:28). When we test ourselves, what are we looking for? First, **faith**. It would be rebellious to come to the signs of the death of Jesus but not be exercising faith in what Jesus has done. Second, **love**. God wants us to keep in mind His entire church. The Corinthians were despising fellow believers. But hostility towards a fellow believer is despising the cross, since Jesus died to bring us and our fellows believers into one body, the true Church of Jesus Christ. Paul has already said, 'Because there is one loaf, we who are many are one body' (10:17). We are to examine not our 'worthiness' but the state of our love towards other believers.

3. **We avoid God's chastening** (11:29–30). There are some differences in the Greek manuscripts here. Some manuscripts read: 'For anyone who eats and drinks **inappropriately** without recognizing the body **of the Lord** eats and drinks judgement to himself.' But the better manuscripts do not have the words 'inappropriately' or 'of the Lord' (which were added because they are found in verse 27). The New International Version (NIV) rightly omits 'unworthily' or 'inappropriately' but mistakenly includes 'of the Lord'. The New American Standard Version (NASV) is better in omitting both phrases. Our verse should be translated, *'For anyone who eats and drinks without recognizing the body eats and drinks judgement to himself'* (11:29). It goes on: *'For this reason many are weak among you and sick and some have died'* (11:30). To ill-treat fellow believers and do so at the Lord's Supper is a very serious matter. It is vital for God's people to recall and recognize God's people, the church, the body of Christ. Failure to do so may well bring upon us divine chastening. So serious is it to damage God's church in this way that some may be prematurely taken to heaven, and lose ministry and reward through their carelessness towards God's people.

4. **We practise self-judgement** (11:31–32). Paul has the remedy to divine discipline. *'But if we judge ourselves, we*

should not be judged (11:31). *And when we are judged by the Lord we are chastened in order that we may not be condemned with the world'* (11:32). The way to avoid unnecessary chastening from God is self-chastening. God is very merciful to those who put aside their wickedness before God does it for them in a more forceful manner. Self-chastening prevents Christians from being 'hurt by' that which the world will know in its full force: God's wrath against sin (Revelations 2:11; Ephesians 5:6–7).

Paul has **final instructions** at the end of this section. (i) They must practise Christian love. *'So, my brothers and sisters, when you come together in order to eat receive one another'* (11:33). They must get rid of their snobbishness and discrimination towards each other and re-establish loving harmony within the fellowship. (ii) They must put aside their misuse of the Lord's Supper. *'If anyone is hungry, let him eat in his house in order that you may not come together for judgement'* (11:34a). They must not use the church as a social occasion where they satisfy their appetite for luxurious meals. If they want to satisfy their appetites in this way let them do it at home! The Lord's Supper must be a spiritual occasion of benefit to all of the congregation at Corinth. (iii) They must get ready for further instructions when Paul comes to them: *'And the other things I will set in order whenever I come'* (11:34b). Paul has more to say to them. They are a congregation being led by an apostle. On quite small matters Paul will give them his instructions in person, but the large-scale teaching he has put into writing – for them and for us.

Chapter 11

The Holy Spirit in Christian Worship
(1 Corinthians 12:1–3)

Paul is dealing with various disorders in the public worship of the church in Corinth. He has had something to say about **men and women in worship** (11:2–16) and the **Lord's Supper** (11:17–34). Now there comes a lengthy section concerning the **gifts of the Holy Spirit** (12:1–14:40).

1. **It is vital to know the teaching concerning this subject**. In the late twentieth and early twenty-first centuries, there has come a revived interest in the gifts of the Spirit all over the world. Christian men and women have generally abandoned the idea that this aspect of scriptural teaching was purely for the first century. But – as in first-century Corinth – it is more vital than ever to know what the Bible teaches. Paul's words to the Corinthians apply to us: *'Now, brothers and sisters, I do not want you to be ignorant concerning spiritual gifts'* (12:1). The Corinthians were in bad need of instruction on this matter. They were certainly experiencing the spiritual gifts. Very much so! They were rich in the gifts of speaking and of knowledge (as 1 Corinthians 1:5 has said). But they were clearly making at least four bad mistakes. (i) They were admiring wildness and noise for its own sake. The more they felt they were being led into excitement, the more they thought this was the work of the Holy Spirit. (ii) They said that – or were behaving as if – some gifts had to be experienced by everyone. (iii) They valued the unintelligible gifts more than the intelligible gifts. (iv) An atmosphere of rivalry and a spirit of superiority was coming into the congregation. So Paul says to them: you need to be well informed about these matters.

2. **Feeling 'led' proves nothing**. Actually the worship at Corinth was quite similar in some ways to the 'worship' they had known in the pagan temples before they had come to faith in Christ. *'You know that when you were gentiles, you were led away to dumb idols, howsoever you might be led'* (12:2). The Corinthians had been involved in lively and noisy worship before they had come to salvation in Christ. That ought to have made them realize that the 'liveliness' of worship is not the most important thing about it. Liveliness is not a proof of the Holy Spirit's presence, because they themselves knew what it was to be lively at a time when it was not the Holy Spirit who was leading them. Feeling 'led' proves nothing. 'Inspired' speaking might not be from the Holy Spirit. Unsaved people feel 'inspired' when they are worshipping idols. The idols are **dumb** and say nothing; the evil spirits behind them are the ones who inspire 'messages' in false religion. So the feeling of being led or inspired does not prove anything. Satan's assistants are clever and can introduce that which is false into public worship.

3. **The important matter is to notice how the Holy Spirit honours Jesus as the risen Lord**. If liveliness and excitement are not proof of the Holy Spirit's presence, what is? Paul goes on to tell us: *'Therefore I make known to you, that no one speaking by the Spirit of God says "Jesus is accursed"; and no one can say "Jesus is Lord" but by the Holy Spirit'* (12:3). Paul is not referring to what happens in the Corinthian meetings (for no one would say 'Jesus is accursed' there). He is rather referring to what happens in pagan meetings. In pagan meetings there was excitement but Jesus was despised. Whatever dishonours Jesus is false; so the idolatrous worship of their past is false, despite being very 'charismatic'. (The phrase 'Jesus is accursed' is very Jewish; Paul is probably expressing pagan statements in his own very Jewish manner.)

On the other hand, where the Spirit is present, the Lordship of Jesus is honoured, and this cannot occur without the working of the Holy Spirit. Of course anyone can say the words 'Jesus is Lord'. What Paul means is that the sincere and public confession that the crucified Lord Jesus Christ is in fact the risen and glorified Lord of the universe is only possible by the powerful working of the Spirit. It was the Holy Spirit who had rescued the Corinthians from paganism and brought them to declare publicly that the Lord Jesus Christ is the divine King of the universe.

This does not mean that acknowledging Jesus is Lord is sufficient to prove that any particular events in the worship are genuine. Paul is only giving a starting point, a broad generalization. The outstanding mark of the Holy Spirit's work is that He brings us **out** of that which dishonours Jesus, and **into** that which proclaims His lordship.

Paul is simply starting his exposition. He has much more to say. Yet he has already introduced us to some important matters.

1. **'Phenomena', excitement and 'feeling inspired' do not prove anything in public worship**. Where the Spirit is at work, there will be excitement and there may well be unusual phenomena, but this does not mean that everything that is exciting and every physical effect is from God or is truly helpful. What begins as a genuine manifestation of the Spirit can be turned into a fleshly piece of sensationalism.[1]

2. **The content of worship is more important than the excitement of worship**. There is excitement in paganism – but it has the wrong content. On the other hand the Spirit exalts and glorifies Jesus in a dynamic and lively way. True Christian worship has both a feeling of liveliness and exalts the crucified Jesus as the risen Lord. We need both the liveliness and the content, but actually the content is the distinguishing mark, more than the liveliness. Satan can promote liveliness; the flesh can promote liveliness – but only the Holy Spirit can exalt Jesus so as to focus our attention on Him. The Holy Spirit brings Jesus to us in His presence, His purity and His power.

Note

[1] See the simplied version of a book by Jonathan Edwards, issued as *God At Work?* (Grace Publications, 1995) and Colin Dye's excellent little book, *Revival Phenomena* (Sovereign World, 1996).

Chapter 12

Unity and Variety

(1 Corinthians 12:4–9)

It is obvious that there was a lot of rivalry and division in Corinth. Paul's next point is that the Holy Spirit produces both variety and unity in the church. *'There are different allocations of gifts but the same Spirit (12:4); there are different allocations of ministries, but the same Lord (12:5); there are different allocations of workings but the same God who works all things in all people'* (12:6).

First of all we notice Paul's Trinitarianism. The Bible teaches that (i) there is only one God; (ii) the Father is God; (iii) God has a divine 'Son'; (iv) the Spirit is divine; (v) the Father is not the Son; (vi) the Father is not the Spirit; (vii) the Son is not the Spirit. These seven facts about God are what we call 'the doctrine of the Trinity'.[1] It is clear that all of this is assumed here by Paul. The entire Godhead – Father, Son and Holy Spirit – are at work in the Church. The entire Godhead – Father, Son and Holy Spirit – give gifts and ministries and workings. We must not break this into three, as if **only** the Spirit gives gifts, and **only** Jesus gives ministries, and **only** the Father gives workings. It does not mean that. It is a Jewish way of talking (the kind of style we often have in the Psalms). It does not mean that the gifts and ministries and workings are parcelled out among the three persons of the Godhead. It means that the Father, the Son and the Spirit (all three) give gifts and ministries and workings (all three).

The emphasis is on the variety of what God does. 'There are different allocations ... different allocations ... different allocations ... '. Three times Paul says it. One great mistake in understanding spiritual gifts is to press people to be the same as each other. Actually God loves variety. Every snowflake, every set of fingerprints, every leaf on every tree, every grain of sand is different from every other. God never makes an exact replica. This is important in Christian worship and life. There can be unusual people who have a ministry which is strikingly unusual. Think of Samson; his spiritual gift was physical strength. Was there anyone else like him? Think of Hosea; he was called to marry a wicked girl. Did anyone else have the same calling? God deals with people very individually, attending to people's gifts one at a time, with immense variety. We are not called to be the same as each other. No one has exactly my gifts. No one has exactly your gifts. Unusual ministries must not be rejected just because they are unusual. No one style of ministry (teaching, singing, 'deliverance', healing) is to dominate everything else. There is room for everything God is doing.

There are 'gifts ... ministries ... workings'. Paul uses three words because he wants to cover the wide variety of what God does. Some Christian activities are 'graciously-given gifts' (*charismata*). Some are 'ministries', ways of serving people. Some are dramatic 'workings', powerful events and signs that a person is enabled to 'work' or to 'perform' for God. The three terms overlap. Everything God does in this way is a gift; it serves; it works. But the three terms stress the many-sided character of the abilities that God gives to His people.

Yet there is to be unity in the Christian church. Despite the great variety, there is 'the same Spirit ... the same Lord ... the same God' who works all things in all people (12:6). Christian people have to protect both the variety of the church and the unity of the church. They have to make sure that people are allowed to be different. They have to make sure people do not drift apart.

Each Christian is given some ability he or she can contribute to the fellowship of God's people. God works all things in all people. He is behind every ability given to His people. He makes sure it all fits together. He gives gifts in a way that ensures His churches move together in the same direction. *'To each Christian is given the manifestation of the Spirit for the common good'* (12:7). How do we know what our gift is? We should not need to ask the question. The Spirit 'manifests' Himself, 'manifests' the gospel and the love of God, through what He gives to each Christian. The question is not: how do I know my gift? The question is: what is the Holy Spirit showing and revealing? We are each in the hands of God. He does things through us surprisingly, sometimes using gifts we did not dream we had.

Paul mentions some of the gifts. *'To one person is given the message of wisdom, through the Spirit; to another the message of knowledge is given by the same Spirit'* (12:8). These two gifts are interpreted in various ways. Some think they refer to short supernatural items of wisdom or knowledge (like Ananias being told of Saul's conversion – Acts 9:11–12). Others (and I agree with them) think 'message' refers to a style of preaching. The important point is the variety ('one ... wisdom, another ... knowledge') and the unity ('through the Spirit ... by the **same** Spirit ... ') that God wants. I hold the view that 'the message of wisdom' is gifted preaching with an emphasis on the practical application of the gospel. The 'message of knowledge' is much the same but shows deeper grasp of the whole counsel of God. I prefer to call the gift first mentioned 'supernatural knowledge'; it is often involved in prophecy as we see interestingly in Luke 22:64. There certainly is such a gift! But it might not be what Paul has in mind here.

'To another person is given faith by the same Spirit' (12:9). 'Faith' is not a reference to saving-faith (for all Christians have that) but to special faith, faith to do something unusual, or to live in an unusual manner. All Christians do not have this gift, but some do. One thinks of George Müller of Bristol who organized orphanages for children and (without ever telling anyone of his needs) was amazingly enabled by God to provide for others. Hudson Taylor, the apostolic pioneer of Christian work in China in the nineteenth century, is another example. But Paul's main point is: God gives spiritual gifts to His people and there is immense variety in the way He does it.

Note

[1] See Eaton, *Experiencing God*, Theology for Beginners series (OM, 1998).

Chapter 13

The Gifts of the Holy Spirit
(1 Corinthians 12:9–12)

Paul is giving a few examples of the gifts of the Holy Spirit. It is not a complete list. There are other gifts mentioned elsewhere which are not mentioned here. And even if they were all combined (to make about twenty-five gifts) it would still not be a complete list. There are spiritual gifts not specially given any name in the New Testament (such as worship-leading, hospitality, ministry among children).

Paul does not make sharp distinctions between dramatic gifts and less dramatic gifts. Some are very sensational (miracles, healings) while others are quiet and inconspicuous (hospitality, intercession, 'helps'). Paul mixes the different kinds of gifts together in his lists. He mentions the more dramatic ones in 1 Corinthians 12:8–10 because that is what the church there was interested in, and they were the gifts causing difficulties. But elsewhere he puts prophecy and service side by side (Romans 12:6–7). Equally he does not divide the gifts into the temporary and the permanent. There is no statement in the New Testament that God will ever cease to give these gifts to His Church.

'To another gifts of healings, by the one Spirit' (12:9b). The word 'gifts' here is plural. There are so many different kinds of healing and different ways in which God heals. People who are frequently used in the healing of others have 'gifts' or 'a gift' of healing.

'To another person is given workings of miracles; to another prophecy; to another discernment of spirit; to another different kinds of tongues; to another interpretation of tongues' (12:10). Again we notice the plural in 'workings of miracles'. It refers

48

to the many different kinds of miracles. One thinks of Jesus calming the sea and controlling the winds. They were not healings but they were miracles.

'Prophecy' is speaking for God in a specially God-given way. There are reasons to think that there are different levels of prophecy. At certain points in the history of the world prophecy accompanied major events of salvation-history (the calling of Abraham, the exodus, the death and resurrection of the Lord Jesus Christ) and at such a time it may have become part of written Scripture. But there are lesser levels of prophecy. Paul expected prophecy in the congregation at Corinth but no Corinthian citizen wrote any part of the Bible.

'Discernment of spirits' could refer to a God-given ability to distinguish the divine and the demonic. Or it could refer to discernment in understanding another person's motivation. Personally I think the man or woman who can do one can normally do the other as well! So it makes no difference. In Jeremiah 28, in a situation where a false prophet was predicting that the King of Babylon was about to be defeated, Jeremiah was prophesying that exile to Babylon was inevitable and Babylon would not be defeated! The gift of discernment of spirits was needed.

'Different kinds of tongues' is non-rational praying. The fact that Paul speaks of 'different kinds' should help us in answering questions about this gift. There are 'different kinds'!

'Interpretation of tongues' is probably not straightforward 'translation' of tongues. It is rather putting into words that can be understood, what another person is praying about in words and noises that cannot be understood.

Paul is mentioning these things to emphasize the great variety of what God does. *'The one and the same Spirit works all these gifts, distributing to each one as He wills'* (12:11). It is vital to note the words 'as He wills'. God is utterly and totally sovereign in allocating the gifts of the Spirit. He can give them, withhold them, vary them, intensify them, reduce them. The church can go through a period when dramatic gifts seem to be withheld. Then there can come a sudden change and the most incredible and unexpected things can happen. He can even make a donkey talk or change the phenomena of the sky so that the day lasts longer! The only rule is that there is no rule.

Now Paul goes on to explain how there can be this amazing variety-and-yet-unity in the Christian church. *'For just as the body is one and has many members, and all the members of the body are one body (although they are many), so it is with Christ'* (12:12).

Paul likes to use the human body as an illustration of unity-and-yet-variety. It is one of the most amazing aspects about the human body. Here I sit in a friend's house in one of the slum suburbs of Nairobi. It is Saturday, almost lunchtime. I am listening to the radio with half an ear. I have a cup of *chai* and a plate of small *mandazi* (doughnuts) not very far away. I can smell the smells of a soon-to-be-served lunch of *ugali* and *dengu* (maize-meal and small peas). My fingers are tapping away on my computer. Occasionally I ask my hosts something ('Hey, why do you think Paul says here, "So it is with Christ" instead of "So it is with the church"?') and I listen to what my friends have to say. I have a slight toothache, which I am uncomfortably conscious of and think about occasionally. My eyes are mostly focused on the computer screen but I occasionally consult my Greek New Testament or some notes on 1 Corinthians. I am sitting cross-legged on a settee with a personal computer in front of me. My heart is beating away (I suppose, but I am not conscious of it). My lungs are going in and out. The blood is going round my body, I hope. I can hear the three young children next door giving their mummy some problems. Many things are going on within the one body – and yet I am really doing only one thing – writing up my exposition of 1 Corinthians 12. **Many things contribute to one thing**. Even the distant sounds of troublesome children are helping me. I like to be with people! I like family noises and communicative people! There is great variety and yet great unitedness in a human body. That is the way it is in the Christian church. Dozens of things go on at the same time. Some you are more conscious of than others. Some are conspicuous; some are obscure and you hardly notice them. But all are necessary. Paul says 'So it is with Christ' instead of

'So it is with the church' because he is conscious that the church-and-Christ together make up 'the body of Christ'. The church is 'Christ' plus His body, but Paul's concentration is on Christ Himself. There are many gifts but the one Head of the church, the Lord Jesus Christ, is taking His church where He wants it to go.

Chapter 14

Baptized by the Spirit
(1 Corinthians 12:13)

The church is 'one body' despite the amazing variety that is to be found within it. *'For by one Spirit we were all baptized into one body, Jews or Greeks, slaves or free, and all were drenched by one Spirit'* (12:13).

1. **First, there are two general matters to be kept in mind**. (i) Paul is not saying anything about water-baptism. Water-baptism certainly does not create the unity of the church. 'Baptize' is a plain and ordinary Greek word meaning 'dip' or 'immerse' or more simply 'place' or 'put'. It is often used where there is no reference to water. (ii) We must keep in mind the possibility that the Greek phrase here is used in more than one way. The phrase is *baptizein en to pneumati* ('to baptize with/by/in the Spirit'). A similar phrase is also used on six occasions in the gospels and Acts (Mark 1:8; Matthew 3:11; Luke 3:16; John 1:33; Acts 1:5; 11:16). We must study these two groups separately before asserting that they are one group with an identical meaning throughout. It is a mistake to assume that all seven verses are 100 per cent identical. Only **after** they have been separately studied may we compare them and **then** see whether they are in fact identical or distinct.

2. **We must consider 1 Corinthians 12:13a in its own context**. The question being discussed in 1 Corinthians 12 is: how does the church get to be 'one body'? The answer is: it is one because *'by one Spirit we were all baptized into one body'*. We are immersed into the body of Christ. Who does the immersing, this placement, into the body of Christ? Looking at this text in its own context, without viewing it in the light of supposed parallels (which were not accessible to the

52

Corinthians), the answer would seem to be: the Holy Spirit does the placement.

3. **It is by the agency of the one Holy Spirit that all believers are placed in the body of Christ**. Eight times in 1 Corinthians 12:3, 4, 8, 9, 11, we have reference to the agency of the Holy Spirit. No one speaking by the agency of the Spirit of God [*en pneumati theou*] says Jesus is accursed; and no one can say 'Jesus is Lord' but by the agency of the Holy Spirit [*en pneumati hagiou*]' (12:3). Verse 4 says gifts come by the agency of the Spirit. Verse 8 tells us that the message of wisdom is given through (*dia*) the Spirit. *Dia* at this point means 'through what the Holy Spirit does in us'; it denotes agency. Verse 8b says the word of knowledge is given according to (*kata*) the same Spirit. *Kata* means 'in accordance with' the Spirit's wishes and methods; it again speaks of the Spirit as the active agent. According to verse 9a faith is given by the same Spirit (*en to auto pneumati*). Verse 9b says healings are given by the one Spirit *(en to heni pneumati)*. Verse 11 says the one and the same Spirit works all of these gifts. The agency of the Spirit has been in view eight times since verse 3, and on four of those occasions the words that Paul uses are some form of *en pneumati*.

When you come to verse 13a there is no special mention of Christ being the agent of the baptism into the body of Christ, and the phrase 'by the Spirit' has just been used explicitly four times in the previous verses, all of them referring to the Spirit's agency. The phrase here is 'by the agency of the Holy Spirit'. It is the same phrase that has already been used in previous verses; there cannot be a change of meaning. The Holy Spirit puts us into Christ and into the body of Christ. The translation should be: '**by** one Spirit we were all baptized into one body'. The Spirit immerses us into the body of Christ.

The New Testament never says that Christ puts us into the body of Christ, or that Christ puts us into Himself. This is not New Testament language. The Spirit puts us into Christ. I have used the word 'put'. I could have used the word 'baptised' or 'placed' or 'immersed'. The Holy Spirit unites us to Christ, and in doing so He places us (puts us, immerses us, baptizes us) into the body of Christ. It is this work of the Spirit that powerfully creates the unity of the church.

4. **Ephesians 4:5 is a parallel verse**. We may compare the teaching here with that of Ephesians 4:5 where again Paul is referring to entities which powerfully and irresistibly create the unity of the church: one body, one Spirit, one hope, one Lord, one faith, one baptism, one God and Father. It is not **water**-baptism that powerfully and irresistibly creates the unity of the church. The 'one baptism' is surely baptism by the Spirit into the body of Christ which has this effect of creating and guaranteeing the church's oneness. This work of the Spirit creates the 'unity of the Spirit' already mentioned in Ephesians 4:3.

5. **Alternative expositions are unconvincing**. Can this exposition above be overthrown? There are several ways in which the attempt is made. Some expositors try to give an unusual interpretation to the word 'all'. 'We all' in 1 Corinthians 12:13 clearly means 'All of us Christians – in Corinth and anywhere else'. It does not mean 'All of us who have experienced something that others have not experienced . . . '. This would imply that those who have not had 'the experience' are not part of the body of Christ.

Another way of avoiding this exposition is to try to give an unusual interpretation of the word 'into'. Some expositors try to make it mean 'with a view to' or 'for the benefit of' or 'to bring us *right* into' (not '*just* into') or 'as already in'. But these interpretations are impossible. One cannot translate the words here as 'for the body' or 'in relation to the body'. Such interpretations are not accepted by any careful and well-informed students of Scripture. Nor can I accept the idea that the word means 'right into' rather than 'just into', indicating completion rather than commencement. Any who consult the most exhaustive and detailed Greek dictionaries will discover that such a meaning with emphasis on '**right** into' is not recognized by any authority in New Testament Greek. The idea of stage-by-stage entry into the body of Christ is not a New Testament way of putting things. We cannot accept any of these ways of getting rid of the word 'into'. 'Into' means 'into'! The Spirit places all believers into the body of Christ.

There were not there before. They become 'in Christ' and at that moment they are put into the body of Christ. The Spirit puts them there as part of their conversion. The unity of the body of Christ as an objective fact is safe and certain. Paul is appealing to this safe and certain fact.

Chapter 15

Drenched by the Spirit

(1 Corinthians 12:13)

6. **The gift of the Spirit overcomes division**. Paul says: *'we were all baptized into one body, Jews or Greeks, slaves or free'*. Regardless of nationality, regardless of culture, regardless of language, regardless of social status, all who have faith in Jesus are equally placed by the Spirit into the body of Christ.

7. **The same words may have different meanings**. It is interesting that those who think 'baptized with the Spirit' always has to have one meaning feel quite differently when they come to another New Testament phrase 'aglow with the Spirit' (*to pneumati zeontes*). This phrase is used in Romans 12:11 and Acts 18:25 in entirely different ways. *'Be set on fire by the Spirit'*, says Paul in Romans 12:11, referring to the Holy Spirit. In Acts 18:25 the similar phrase (*zeon to pneumati*) says that Apollos was 'fervent in spirit'. It refers to natural temperament, but the wording is virtually identical to that in Romans 12:11. In Acts 18:25 Apollos had not received the Spirit when he was said to be fervent in spirit, but Romans 12:11 is agreed to refer to the Holy Spirit. Writers who insist that *baptizein en to pneumati* cannot have two meanings invariably give two meanings to *to pneumati zeontes*! They argue that one set of phrases must be identical but take the other set of phrases to refer to different things! These expositors tend to have some preconceived ideas when they come to 1 Corinthians 12:13a and the other six texts, but a more impartial judgement is at work in interpreting Acts 18:25 in relation to Romans 12:11.

8. **A question might be asked at this point**: Is the baptism into the body of Christ by the Holy Spirit a conscious experience?

Is it as vivid an experience as that mentioned in the other six verses containing the same phraseology?

There are those who want to maintain that the 'Spirit-baptism' of 1 Corinthians 12:13 is **not** an 'experience'. Then they go on to say that the six other references must be interpreted similarly and there is therefore no such thing as an 'experience' of Spirit-baptism. The seven verses (they say) refer to the one-and-only baptism with the Spirit. It is not vivid and unforgettable but is below the level of consciousness, and cannot in any way be 'felt'. It is an 'event' but not an 'experience' (as a famous theologian once said to me). It is a continuation of what happened on the Day of Pentecost but it does not involve the kind of experience that people knew on that day. There is no such thing (it is said) as a Pentecostal-type 'experience' which ought to be known by all Christians.

There are those who want to say that the 'Spirit-baptism' of 1 Corinthians 12:13 **is indeed** based on a powerful experience. Then they go on to say that the six other references must be interpreted similarly and therefore 'becoming a Christian' is a powerful and charismatic experience. The seven verses (they say) refer to the one-and-only baptism with the Spirit. It is the *experience* of receiving power, of emotional prayerfulness, of direct awareness that God is our Father. It is a foretaste of heaven. Here in 1 Corinthians 12:13 (they say) it is the *experience* of being powerfully introduced to the gifts of the Spirit within the body. Those who take 1 Corinthians 12:13 in this way imply that those who have not had this experience are not in the body of Christ, or that they are not *fully* in the body of Christ.

Both of these views have one thing in common. They both interpret seven texts as referring to the same spiritual reality. One group says it is not based in experience; the other group says it is. But there is a third approach, and this is the one that I believe in.

There are those who want to say that the 'Spirit-baptism' of 1 Corinthians 12:13 is not described in precisely the same way as the 'Spirit-baptism' of the six other texts. The 'Spirit-baptism' of the six references is obviously a vibrant experience as well as being an objective event. In the descriptions of receiving the Spirit (identified with being baptized with the Spirit) the focus is very much on 'experience'. But in the 'Spirit-baptism' of 1 Corinthians 12:13a, Paul is concerned much more with the objective side of the matter. No doubt experience is involved there also (as 12:13b suggests) but the focus is not on the experience; it is on the objective event which irresistibly brings the believer into the body of Christ. So 1 Corinthians 12:13a must refer to something different (or at least have a different emphasis) in comparison with the other six references. There are thus two differences between 1 Corinthians 12:13 and the six other texts that use similar language. One is an experience; the other has to be 'reckoned' (as Romans 6:11 puts it). The agent of one is said to be Christ; the agent of the other is the Spirit. This verse in 1 Corinthians 12:13 must not be interpreted via the six texts in the gospels and Acts. And the gospels and Acts must not be interpreted via 1 Corinthians 12:13.

Next Paul says: *'and all were drenched by one Spirit'* (12:13). We may dismiss interpretations that (i) think that 12:13a and 12:13b both refer to water-baptism, (ii) those who think that the first phrase refers to water-baptism and the second to confirmation, or (iii) those who think that the first phrase refers to water-baptism and the second to the Lord's Supper. I reject also (iv) the idea that *both* halves of the verse refer to a Pentecostal-type experience of the Spirit which somehow relates to the body of Christ. (v) A fifth approach takes the view that the first phrase refers to conversion (perhaps an aspect of conversion not based on experience) but the **second** phrase refers to a distinct post-conversion experience of the Holy Spirit or to an outpouring of the gifts of the Spirit. I more or less agree with this (although if such an experience is 'post-conversion' it is very unusual by New Testament standards).

If (as I have said) verse 13a focuses on the objective fact that the gift of the Spirit brings the believer into the body of Christ at the time of conversion, it seems that verse 13b is based much more on experience: *'and all were drenched by one Spirit'* (12:13). Generally speaking all New Testament Christians experienced a consciously-known outpouring of the Spirit. It is not the **experience** that puts us into the body of Christ, but nevertheless New Testament Christians did from the very earliest days of their salvation enjoy powerful blessings of the Holy Spirit. The Holy Spirit placed them into Christ at the moment of their conversion and immediately, or quite soon after, they experienced powerful workings of the Holy Spirit in their life – including being given the gifts of the Holy Spirit.

Chapter 16

The Body

(1 Corinthians 12:14–23)

Paul emphasizes his main point again. *'For also the body is not one member but many'* (12:14). Now Paul begins to work out the implications of this variety-and-unity in the Christian church.

His first principle is: because of this variety-and-unity nature of the Christian church **no Christian can opt out of the body of Christ.** *'If the foot should say "Because I am not a hand, I am not a part of the body," that would not make it any less a part of the body* (12:15). The picture of a body with talking parts is a funny one, but very illuminating. Imagine a foot that would rather like to be a hand. 'The hand can do things that I cannot do,' says the foot. 'It can write. It can use tools. It can greet other people. I wish I were a hand.' Then the foot gets overwhelmed with self-pity. 'There is nothing worthwhile for me to do. I don't really belong to this body.'

And the ear does the same thing. *'And if the ear should say, "Because I am not an eye, I am not a part of the body," it is not any the less a part of the body'* (12:16). 'The eye is cleverer than me,' says the ear. 'It can distinguish colours, but I can't hear the difference between blue and red. The eye can see the moon but I can't hear the moon. The eye can do things I can't do. I wish I were an eye. I don't think I am needed in this body because the eye can do things I can't do.'

'What nonsense!' says Paul. 'The foot is part of the body. The ear is part of the body. They cannot pull out.' The point of Paul's illustration is that some people within the church of Jesus start opting out because their gifts are not great enough for them. Because they do not have the great gifts of others (as they see it) they get full of self-pity and want to pull out altogether. Paul says: you can't pull out of the body of Christ. God put you there. You are there whether you like it or not. Your self-pity does not change anything.

A second principle is: **every member of the body is in fact valuable in one way or another**. The body would be weakened if a foot were missing. The ear is part of the body and can do things the eye cannot do – such as enjoy good music. *'If the whole body were an eye, where would be the hearing? If the whole were an ear, where would be the sense of smell?'*

Actually you are needed. The body will lose something if you do not play a part in it. It would be a very weird kind of body that was entirely one gigantic ear, or one gigantic eye. The foot does things that the hands and eyes cannot do.

Paul's words rebuke an inferiority complex. The person who thinks he or she has lesser gifts must make no mistake here. The gifts may indeed be less important but they are needed. Let every foot get on with doing what a foot can do. Let every ear get on with doing what an ear can do. The hands and eyes of the body need them.

God has arranged the body of Christ as He wishes. Paul says: *'But now in point of fact God has placed the members, each one of them, in the body, just as He wished'* (12:18). God brings great order, variety and balance within the human body – and also within the church. Any Christian who tries to exercise a gift he or she does not have is in fact rebelling against God's arrangement of His people. Any Christian who refuses to use a gift (perhaps wanting to do something that would be more admired) is equally rebellious.

No one gift may dominate over the body of Christ. Sometimes people want simply one gift to be used. But Paul says: *'And if they were all one member where would the body be?'* (12:19). If everything is teaching, that part of the church ceases to be a varied body. If a congregation becomes a kind of healing-cult and only the gift of healing is admired, that part of the church ceases to be a varied body. *'But now there are many members, but one body'* (12:20). There is great variety but unity at the same time.

Every person is needed in the church of Jesus Christ. Paul says: *'And the eye cannot say to the hand, "I have no need of you" or again the head to the feet, "I have no need of you"'* (12:21). There are less conspicuous gifts in the church – cheerfulness, a skill at attending to detail, an instinctive mercy towards the needy, an ability to restore the fallen. These gifts are needed too. *'On the contrary,'* says Paul, *'it is much truer that the members of the body which seem to be weaker are necessary* (12:22); *and those members of the body which we think to be less honourable, on those we give more abundant honour, and our unseemly members come to have more abundant seemliness* (12:23), *whereas our seemly members have no need of it'* (12:24a). Some parts of the body are conspicuous (the face, the overall figure). Some parts are kept covered (Paul is thinking of the sexual parts of the body). But actually the covered parts are very vital and need care. Some gifts get a lot of attention: powerful preaching, dramatic miracles of healing. But the more conspicuous people need the less conspicuous people. What chaotic lives a lot of preachers would be living if it were not for an almost unnoticed secretary. No member may be independent of the others.

Chapter 17

Sympathy in the Body of Christ
(1 Corinthians 12:24–31)

God's will for His entire worldwide Church is that we have much sympathy and respect for each other. Every part of the body of Christ (which is the total number of those who have living faith in Jesus) is necessary for the life of the churches.

The weaker and less well-known parts of the body of Christ actually should receive greater care and attention. Paul says: *'But God has so combined the body, giving more abundant honour to that member which was less gifted* (12:24), *that there should be no division in the body, but that the members should have the same care for one another'* (12:25). Here we have God's plan concerning the way we should treat each other. God's will is that the less gifted person should receive a lot of attention. This does not of course mean that such a person is pushed into high office in the church, but that some trouble is taken to see that the person who is less conspicuously gifted is helped to find his or her place in the life of the body. When Paul says, 'God has so combined the body...', he is not saying that it always happens, but he is saying that this is God's will, God's plan. If God gets His way, this is what happens. The less gifted are not made to feel obscure or unloved. *'And if one member suffers, all the members suffer with it; if one member is honoured, all the members rejoice with it'* (12:26). God arranges the body so as to bring harmony (12:24b–26). This is the way He wants us to live within the churches.

Paul is thinking of the 'universal' or worldwide Church. Yet he is insisting that they must regard themselves as being as much a part of that worldwide Church as anyone else anywhere. *'Now you are Christ's body and each one of you is a part of that body'* (12:27). We are to realize who we are in the Lord Jesus Christ.

Paul now presses on to work out the implications of what he has said. *'And God has appointed in the church first apostles, second prophets, third teachers, then workers of miracles, then healers, helpers, administrators, speakers in various kinds of tongues'* (12:28). He is now specifying what he meant when he spoke of this great variety. Three kinds of people are the main leaders in the Church. Apostles (church planters, pioneers and leaders of major ministries) are the most useful ministries in the Church. Prophets come next; they are preachers with unusual power in giving direction for this very moment in this very situation that we are in now. They do not have the organizational skills that apostles have. Teachers come next. They have skill in bringing the entire church to understand and apply the message of the gospel. Their preaching is not quite so 'directed-to-this-very-occasion'.

Other ministries are not numbered, and there is no further grading of importance. There are: workers of miracles, healers, helpers, administrators, speakers in various kinds of tongues.

But Paul is still concerned about the variety of the church. *'Are all apostles? Are all prophets? Are all teachers?'* (12:29). *Do all work miracles? Do all possess gifts of healing? Do all speak with tongues? Do all interpret?'* (12:30). Obviously the answer to these questions is: no! Are all apostles? No. Are all prophets? No. Are all teachers? No. Paul is discouraging people who want to be apostles or prophets or teachers – when that is not the calling of God upon their lives.

We might be specially interested in the question, *'Do all speak with tongues?'* His answer is clearly: no. But it must be remembered that he is referring to the public life of the worshipping congregation when he says this. In Romans 8:26 he takes it for granted that there will be a kind of non-rational praying that is typical of all Christians. Both 1 Corinthians 12:30 and Romans 8:26 must be taken into our thinking. Certainly not every Christian should covet to be a tongues-speaker in public worship. But every Christian should know something of the inarticulate sighs and syllables given to us by the Holy Spirit. It is a form of praying that cannot be understood. Romans 8:26 is either the same as 'tongues' or it is very similar. Certainly, when a Christian prays there is more to it than simply speaking rational words that can be understood, but not everyone is called to express such inarticulate sighs and syllables into public worship, and those who do so must take care to follow the guidance that Paul is about to give.

So Paul concludes this sub-section. *'But earnestly desire the higher gifts'* (12:31a). What are the 'higher gifts? He has told us: first apostles, second prophets, third teachers. They are forms of communicating the Word of God in ways that can be easily understood, and so building the churches in faith and love.

Next Paul tells us how to seek the gifts: *'And I will show you an excellent way'* (12:31b). It is a mistake to translate 'a more excellent way'. There is no 'more' in the Greek. Paul is not actually saying love is more excellent than gifts. It might be true but it is not what he is saying. He is not putting down gifts in favour of love. He is showing the way in which the gifts are to be sought. In putting it in this way he is showing us that we might be given more than we have at present. We have gifts for the body of Christ already, but God is willing to give us more. A new convert is gifted immediately, but he probably will not become an apostle immediately. There are gifts to be sought, and Paul will show us a very excellent way to do it.

Chapter 18

The Supremacy of Love

(1 Corinthians 13:1–4)

Paul has put forward general principles concerning the gifts of the Holy Spirit (in 1 Corinthians 12). He intends to go into detail concerning two particular gifts (in 1 Corinthians 14). But in-between he spends a chunk of his valuable writing-space speaking of the need for Christian love in the church. It is interesting that it is in connection with the gifts of the Spirit that he says so much about Christian love. Gifts of the Spirit can damage love, and stir up a lot of jealousy and disagreement in the church. Paul wants them to think long and hard about love before he goes on into his thoughts about tongues and prophecy.

'If I speak with human tongues and with the tongues of angels, but have not love, I have become only a noisy gong or a clanging symbol (13:1). *And if I have the gift of prophecy, and know all mysteries and have full knowledge; and if I have faith so as to remove mountains, but do not have love, I am nothing* (13:2). *And if I give all my possessions in order to feed the poor, and give away my body to be burned, but have not love, I gain nothing'* (13:3). Four times he uses the word 'if'. '**If** I speak with tongues ... **if** I have the gift of prophecy ... **if** I have faith ... **if** I give all my possessions ...'.

Love is greater than the greatest of gifts. 'If I speak with human tongues and with the tongues of angels, but have not love, I have become only a noisy gong or a clanging symbol' (13:1). Miraculous gifts of the Spirit were much admired in Corinth, but Paul says Christian love is so much greater that even the most admired gifts are worthless in comparison. God

asks us to have love, much more than He asks us to speak in
tongues.

**Love is greater than the greatest styles of speaking and of
knowledge**. 'And if I have the gift of prophecy, and know all
mysteries and have full knowledge...' (13:2a). How much
people admire gifted speakers. How much people want to
speak with words given by God Himself. Paul will say later
that prophecy is to be sought more than all the other gifts
(14:39). How much people value knowledge, understanding
and intellectual ability or God-given insight. Yet, says Paul,
we can have all of this and be nothing in spiritual stature
because of our lack of love (13:1).

Love is greater than the greatest achievements. 'And if I ...
have full knowledge; and if I have faith so as to remove
mountains, but do not have love, I am nothing' (13:2b).
'Moving mountains' is a proverbial expression for doing the
impossible. The most impossible task to move is a mountain.
In Hebrew they used to speak about 'the everlasting hills'!
They were the most unmovable thing around. But even the
greatest achievements can be done without love.

Love is greater than the greatest achievements. Paul says:
'And if I give all my possessions in order to feed the poor, and
give away my body to be burned, but have not love, I gain
nothing' (13:3). We might think that giving away our possessions or sacrificing our very life is the greatest way there can
be of showing love. Paul says something different. He says
people can show what seems to be the greatest generosity or
make the greatest sacrifices but still be love-less. In such a case
Christians lose their reward. They 'gain nothing' for their
great sacrifices.

So what is this love? Paul begins to describe the kind of love
he has in mind. *'Love is patient; love is kind.'* It is a basic
description. Negatively, love is patient. Positively, love is
kind.

Patience is slowness to act. Love slows us down when we
are over-inclined to act too hastily. It is slow to anger, slow to
speak, slow to act in a way that will hurt the other person. It
does not make hasty judgements or jump to conclusions
before it has adequately considered the facts. Love makes us

act more cautiously. Hate jumps into situations too quickly. Love is self-restraining. It puts up with situations that arouse our resentment. It acts slowly when receiving from others dishonesty, unfairness, or unreasonable demands. Christ is the greatest example. He constantly faced antagonism and slander, but was slow to do anything about it.

Positively, love is kind. It actively goes out in kindness towards the other person. It takes trouble to be a means of blessing to the other person. It helps the hungry and the sick. Just as God makes His sun to shine upon the evil and the good, so the kind person has a warm heart towards all people everywhere. Kindness is prayerful about others. It prays for enemies. It is not motivated by money. 'Do good and lend,' said Jesus, 'expecting for nothing to come back to you' (Luke 6:35). Kindness includes hospitality and generosity to others. 'He that sows sparingly shall reap sparingly,' said Paul (2 Corinthians 9:6).

Paul asks us to make the deliberate choice of valuing love above enthusiasm for charismatic life, above doctrine and intellectual skills, above great practical endeavours. He asks us to think of ourselves as spiritual weaklings and nobodies unless we are conscious that God is leading us into the pathways of love. We might gather a lot of attention to ourselves, as does a noisy gong or a clanging symbol. People might be impressed by our many skills and gifts. We may gain a reputation for sacrifice and dedication. But only love will bring us the approval of God. Only to people of love will Jesus say, 'Well done!' God is love. We are only godly men and women if we become like Him in His loving patience and loving kindness. The challenge before us is a great one.

Chapter 19

The Love That Overcomes
(1 Corinthians 13:5–8a)

Paul is in the process of describing Christian love. He has given a basic negative-and-positive description (13:4) and now he goes on to speak of the things that love will not do. *'Love is not jealous, love does not boast, it is not arrogant* (13:4b). *Love does not behave disgracefully, it does not seek its own, is not provoked, does not take into account a wrong suffered'* (13:5).

Love is free from jealousy. There is a spirit of rivalry deep in the nature of all of us. It is a sin affecting close relationships that we often fail to see in ourselves and hate to admit. It was a problem for Joseph and his brothers, and for Paul and his fellow preachers (see Philippians 1:15). Love faces the evil and overcomes, finding contentment in Christ.

Love is free from boastfulness. There is a sequence in this description:

Putting up with the bad and the weak: love is patient.

Wanting the good: love is kind.

Enjoying the good in others: love is not jealous.

Not despising the person who has less: love does not boast.

Boasting refers to the way we talk. We like to feel superior to others, so we talk about how well we are doing. It prompts the jealousy of others and puts them down. Love sees how hateful it all is and does not do it.

Love is free from scornfulness. Pride leads to conflict and scornful attitudes. We easily become hostile to the other person, and feel superior. Unlike Job who came to say, *'I despise myself and repent in dust and ashes'*, we become 'puffed up', think a great deal of ourselves and see nothing to repent over. As a result we are totally loveless.

69

Love is free from self-centredness. Love does not behave disgracefully, says Paul. He is thinking of the self-centred behaviour that was to be found in Corinth, such as the women who were ambitious to act like men, and the people who misused the Lord's Supper in their own self-centred interests. But love is free from rude behaviour of this kind.

Love is not self-seeking. Love is the opposite of selfishness. Sin is basically self-centredness, self-love, but love reverses this selfishness. Love leads a person to be public-spirited and sympathetic. It leads us to give up our own interests and concerns for the sake of others.

Love is free from unrestrained anger. If, as Paul says, the roots of sin in us are pride and self-centredness, their result is an angry, vindictive spirit. But love overcomes these ingrained weaknesses.

Love is free from resentment. It does not take into account a wrong suffered and takes little notice when it is ill-treated. It does not 'reckon the wrong', says the Greek more literally. This is what the love of Jesus is. In Jesus God does not reckon our sins against us (2 Corinthians 5:19). That is what love is like. We remember Jesus' prayer that His enemies would be forgiven (Luke 23:34).

Now, in another basic negative-and-positive description (like 13:4a), he speaks of what love takes delight in. *'It does not rejoice in unrighteousness but rejoices with the truth'* (13:6). The loving person refuses to take delight in any kind of evil, whether it be war, ill-treatment of the underprivileged, the fall of an enemy, some misdeed in the family or in the office. It never gloats. It is never glad when there is a fall or a failure of some kind. Love rejoices in every kind of truth and every aspect of truth. It loves the gospel. It loves mercy and compassion and forgiveness and encouragement. All-round goodness is love's delight.

This sub-unit closes with a fourfold description. *'Love always endures, always believes, always hopes, always perseveres'* (13:7). This description tells us how love faces difficulties from other people. It always endures. It bears up under the distress of hate or opposition or painful failure in another person. It always trusts. Love is the opposite of having a sceptical spirit. It never loses faith in the possibility that God will change the situation. Love always hopes. It is optimistic about the other person, without being gullible. Even if the situation is terrible now, love hopes for better things in the future. It maintains the hope that God will change the situation. It loves the other person enough to hope that change is coming. Love always perseveres. It does not easily give up. The words *'Love never fails'* (1 Corinthians 13:8a) form both the conclusion of this point, as well as being the starting point of the next section 13:8–13. In part they mean that love never gives up. Even when rebuffed and rejected, it goes on loving. Even when it finds no response in the other person it does not fall to the ground.

It has often been noted that Paul's words could easily be a description of Jesus. God is love, and anyone who sees Jesus sees God. Jesus is the image of God. We know what God is like by looking at Jesus. Jesus was utterly patient and came to show us God's kindness. He was never jealous, never boastful, never arrogant. Every word of Paul's description could be applied to Him. More than anyone He bears with us and gives us everlasting life to let us know that He always has hopes for us. More wonderfully than anything He always perseveres. He never leaves us nor forsakes us. Jesus is love. God's love is made flesh in Jesus.

No one can have a totally happy conscience after reading 1 Corinthians 13:4–7. We are the opposite of 1 Corinthians 13:4–7 at every point. But love overcomes, and for 'the person who overcomes' there are great promises. The image of God appears in us as we grow to love people the way God loved us, in and through the Lord Jesus Christ.

Chapter 20

The Partial and the Perfect
(1 Corinthians 13:8–13)

'Love never fails,' says 1 Corinthians 13:8a. It seems to bring to an end the little unit in 13:4–7, but it also opens up a new thought. Love is eternal; it will never end. Anything that does the will of God lasts forever, and love certainly is doing the will of God.

Paul now develops this thought. *'Love never fails. If there are prophecies, they will come to an end, or if there are tongues they will cease, or if there is knowledge it will come to an end'* (13:8). Love is eternal; the gifts of the Spirit are not. Paul does not yet say when the 'cessation' will take place. It will soon become clear that he has in mind the end of the world. The implication is that the gifts of the Spirit will continue **until** the end of the world, but they will not continue after that. We shall not be giving prophecies in heaven. Nor shall we be talking in tongues in heaven. Anyone who lives to display their wonderful spiritual gifts needs to remember: it is the amount of love we have shown that will have eternal significance. The amount of gifts we have used will not have eternal significance. The Corinthians admired prophecy and gifts of tongues and deep spiritual insight. It is fine to admire the grace of God in giving gifts, but the gifts themselves will not last forever. Only the way we have shown love.

Paul goes on to explain why the gifts are not eternal. *'For we have only partial knowledge, and we prophesy with only a partial view of what is happening* (13:9). *But when the perfect situation comes, what is partial is abolished'* (13:10). Paul is clearly contrasting our position in this gospel-age with what will be true after the coming of the Lord Jesus Christ. (The old idea that 'the perfect situation' refers to the coming of the twenty-seven books of the New Testament is now almost entirely abandoned; it never was a very natural interpretation. Paul never says anything anywhere about the New Testament. It would have been a remarkable prophecy if he ever did, and he is certainly not speaking about canonical books of Scripture here.)

He uses an illustration. *'When I was a child, I used to speak as a child, I used to think with a childish mentality, I used to reason in a childlike manner* (13:11), *but when I became a full-grown man, I put aside the things of childhood'* (13:12). This is Paul's way of expressing the very great contrast between what we are now and what we shall be in our final resurrected glory. Our present situation is babyhood compared to what is about to come to us in our final glory. These gifts of the Spirit – wonderful though they are – are only like playing with toys! We are not to get excited about them as if they were going to last forever. All of the gifts are to be viewed in this way, including 'knowledge', supernatural insight. Paul is not saying that only tongues is for the baby-stage. All of the gifts are like a baby's toys compared to the full-knowledge of God that will be ours in the final glory. We are allowed to get excited about love. We can get excited about the honour and glory of God. Those things will last forever. But the gifts of the Spirit – which characterize our spiritual infancy here in this world – are just helpful to us for our few years of babyhood here in this life.

'For now we see through a mirror indirectly, but then face to face. Now I know things only partially but then I shall fully know just as I will also be fully known' (13:13a). At the moment our knowledge is not as full as it will one day be. It is like the difference between looking in a mirror and looking at a person face to face. The mirrors of ancient Corinth were of high quality, but they did not enable the whole person to be perfectly and fully seen. So our knowledge of God, aided by gifts of the Spirit, is quite good and it is real. But there is something much greater and better that is coming to us. Our present knowledge of God will seem quite babyish once we get to know God as we shall do in the final glory. One day we

shall know God in a manner that is similar to the way He knows us – *'just as I will also be fully known'* (13:13a). God does not need prophecy or gifts of the Spirit to know us. He knows us directly and fully. One day we shall know Him in the same way and we shall no longer need the gifts of the Spirit.

'And now at this time faith, hope, love, these three things, are continuing. But the greatest of these is love' (13:13b). Paul has been contrasting the present age with final glory. Now he comes to what is important in the present age. There are things that are more important than the gifts of the Spirit. Faith, hope and love are the three most vital characteristics of the Christian life. More important than anything else is that we continue in trust of God, continue in expecting Him to fulfil all of His promises in our lives and in His church, and continue to show love to everyone everywhere. Among these three the greatest is love. All three continue now, but one day faith and hope will disappear. Faith will be replaced by sight. Hope will be replaced by fulfilment. Only love will go on forever and ever.

We remember that Paul is showing us an excellent way, a way to seek the gifts of the Spirit. We seek the gifts of the Spirit in faith. We seek them with hope, in the expectation that God will work powerfully in His church. These are the things that will **continue**. Yet even more, we seek the gifts of the Spirit in love. Love will help us use the gifts in the right way even now. Then one day the gifts will fade away, and love will continue forever.

Chapter 21

Prophecy and Tongues

(1 Corinthians 14:1–5)

Paul comes to discuss the two gifts that were clearly causing some difficulties in Corinth. He asks the Corinthians to seek both the gifts of the Spirit and the life of love. *'Follow after love, and eagerly desire the spiritual gifts, especially that you may prophesy'* (14:1). Prophecy is speaking for God with special help being given even in one's very words. God 'puts words in the mouth'. It is clear that there are various levels and perhaps various kinds of prophecy.

What then is the gift of tongues? It is a form of non-rational prayer. It is a prayer that does not use ordinary language. *'For anyone who speaks in a tongue does not speak to people, but to God'* (14:2a). No one understands it, not even the one who is praying. In the gift of tongues we are praying to God alone. *'For no one understands, but he speaks mysteries by the Spirit'* (14:2).

Various questions are often asked. **Is it ecstatic?** The answer is: there are different kinds of tongues and one cannot make rules about these things. There is certainly no loss of control. The person may be excited but may not be. The person may go into a kind of trance (like Peter in Acts 10:10) but that is not a necessary part of speaking in tongues. **Are the languages real earthly languages?** Might the person be praying in Urdu or Cantonese or Serbo-Croation but not realize it? Again I answer: there are no rules on the matter. The 'tongues' on the Day of Pentecost were certainly known languages. Modern tongues are certainly not generally any earthly languages that could be recognized by a linguistic expert. One occasionally hears stories of people recognizing a language when someone else is praying in tongues, but such stories are not well documented and are rare. **How supernatural are they?** Again there may be various levels of the extent to which tongues is produced by God. On the Day of Pentecost the tongues were very supernatural; they were sheer miracle. Modern tongues are obviously less supernatural. Tongues-speakers generally only use sounds in their own language. A German tongues-speaker does not generally use English 'th' when speaking in tongues. A European tongues-speaker is not generally heard using Swahili 'ng'. A non-Frenchmen is not heard using French 'u'. A Kenyan tongues-speaker is not heard using the English short 'i'. And so on. Their tongues can often be started at will. All of this is clearly somewhat non-miraculous. (This is not a problem. The same questions can be asked about preaching. Some prophetic speaking for God is highly miraculous. Yet preachers use some natural abilities as well, and most preaching is not exclusively miraculous!) **Does it have any meaning?** Yes. The 'tongues' can sometimes be 'interpreted'. In general the meaning is perhaps not known but that is not to say it has no meaning or content. It does have content.

Paul's main point in 1 Corinthians 14:3–5 is that prophecy is superior to tongues because it is better for the congregation to be given a message they can understand than one they can't. The tongues-speaker speaks mysteries by the Spirit. *'But anyone who prophesies speaks to people for their strengthening and encouragement and comfort'* (14:3). Prophecy is helpful to people because it can be understood. Tongues is different. *'The person who speaks in a tongue edifies himself, but he who prophesies edifies the church'* (14:4). Tongues strengthens the person praying in tongues even though he or she does not know exactly what is being prayed. But there is very little strengthening of others if someone else is praying incomprehensively. As a personal gift Paul values the gift of tongues highly. *'I would like everyone of you to speak in tongues ... '*. But in public it has little value. *'I would like everyone of you to speak in tongues, but I would rather have you prophesy. The person who prophesies is greater than the one who speaks in tongues, unless he interprets so that the church may be edified'*

(14:5). Only when the tongues is explained to others may it have a strengthening effect. But prophecy is different. It is speaking for God in a way that people can understand, and with special help including God-given words.

I have said that it is clear that there are various levels and perhaps various kinds of prophecy. In the Old Testament times, from Moses to Malachi, there were men and women who were mouthpieces for God in an extraordinary way. They were inspired in a word-by-word manner. They gave inspired interpretations of the mighty acts of God. Some of this prophecy became part of our Old Testament. We regard it as part of the infallible written Word of God. But the New Testament gift of prophecy is much lower and lesser than what we know from the Old Testament. In the New Testament apostles had higher authority than prophets. Most New Testament prophecy is of a much lesser kind than what we know from the Old Testament. The prophecy given 'by means of the Spirit' in Acts 21:4 was not treated by Paul with the kind of respect he would have given to the words of (let us say) Isaiah. The prophecy of Acts 21:10–11 did not have the kind of exact accuracy expected of an Old Testament prophet.

Prophecy is speaking for God with special help being given even in one's very words. Such a gift is not infallible. It cannot give new doctrines. Prophecies need testing and should not be simply accepted. They should be tested by their being compared with previous revelations. God will not contradict what He has already said, especially within Scripture. Sometimes a word from God through another person is warm, encouraging, and obviously in harmony with Scripture. The greatest prophecies of all are prophetic expositions of Scripture where the prophecy has a firmly biblical base, yet has an appropriateness and is very immediate and contemporary. Then we know we are hearing from God. It is the greatest gift, greater than the gift of tongues.

Chapter 22

Making Sure to be Understood

(1 Corinthians 14:6–19)

Paul presses upon his Corinthian friends the need of comprehensibility, in the public use of the gifts of the Spirit, for the message to be clearly understood. *'And now, brothers and sisters, if I come to you speaking with tongues, what benefit shall I be to you unless I speak to you by revelation or by knowledge or in a prophecy or in teaching?'* (14:6). Any spoken ministry must bring a **comprehensible** revelation or a **comprehensible** piece of spiritual knowledge. It may be some kind of inspired prophecy or a more 'ordinary teaching'. But unless it can be understood it is of no value.

1. **First he puts the point in a series of illustrations**. His first illustration concerns musical instruments. *'And when they make a sound even lifeless instruments, such as the flute or harp, if they do not give distinct notes, how will anyone know what is being played on the flute or played on the harp?'* (14:7). The point is the same. If the other person is to be affected or to enjoy the music there must be some kind of clarity in the playing of the instrument. Intelligent music brings pleasure.

Then he makes the same point in another way by using the example of the bugle in an army. *'And if the bugle gives an indistinct sound, who will get ready for battle?'* (14:8). The bugle is intended to have an impact upon the soldier. It rouses him; it sends a message to him. But only a clear sound will produce the desired effect. The same is true in the Christian church. A clear sound must be heard in the sharing of God's word if the church is to be roused to action. A flow of syllables from the tongues-speaker that makes no sense, will not help anyone much, valuable though it may be to the person himself. Only intelligent playing of the bugle will get an army ready for action.

'It must be this way with you also, when you use your tongue. If you do not give a message that is easily understood, how will anyone know what is said?' Paul applies his illustrations to the Corinthians. He speaks very forcefully. *'You will be speaking into the air!'* he says (14:9).

His next illustration concerns the use of different languages in the world. Corinth was a seaport and a gathering-place of many different peoples. Many languages would be heard there. *'There are I don't know how many kinds of voices in the world, and none of them is without meaning* (14:10). *But unless I personally understand the meaning of what is said to me, I am a foreigner to the speaker and the speaker is a foreigner to me'* (14:11). Paul is not saying that 'tongues' is just another language. He is using an analogy, not an example. To communicate properly people must be able to understand what is being said. Something similar applies in the case of tongues.

He comes to a vital conclusion: *'So it must be this way with you also, because you are eager for spiritual gifts. Seek to build up the church, in order that you may make good progress'* (14:12). The Corinthians are to seek to use spiritual gifts in a way that communicates to everyone and builds up the church in spiritual understanding and obedience.

2. **Then Paul presses home his point more forcefully** (14:13–19). It seems that the Corinthians favoured incomprehensible wildness in their meetings. People sometimes make the mistake of thinking that a kind of chaotic wildness is a mark of the Holy Spirit's special presence. It is not so. There is a difference between liveliness and chaos.

'Therefore let the one who speaks in a tongue pray that he or she may interpret what is said' (14:13). The gift of interpretation has been mentioned in 12:10, 30 and 14:5. It is putting into comprehensible words what is being said incomprehensibly. It is not necessarily 'straight' translation (which might not be possible if the tongues does not have a language-structure typical of ordinary languages). Paul's instruction

implies that one might have more than one gift, and it implies that new gifts may be given.

'*For if I pray in a tongue, my spirit prays but my mind is unfruitful*' (14:14). Paul uses himself as an example. Praying with tongues involves the human spirit, but does not involve the mind. When Paul prays in tongues the mind is 'unfruitful' – dormant, making no contribution, uninvolved, making no intellectual effort. '*What then? I shall pray with the spirit and I shall pray with the mind also*' (14:15a). Paul will make use of two types of praying. He is ready to pray in tongues in a church meeting, but only if (having prayed that he may interpret) he is then able to pray or explain what he has prayed in plain language. The same is true if he is singing with the gift of tongues. '*I shall sing with the spirit and I shall sing with the mind also*' (14:15b). It is pleasant to imagine Paul singing solo in the Corinthian congregation, first in tongues, and then in Greek which they could understand.

In public worship everyone must be able to understand what is going on. '*Otherwise if you worship God with the spirit only, how will the one who is in the position of not being able to understand say the "Amen" at your giving of thanks, since he does not know what you are saying?*' (14:16). The Christian who does not know what this tongue is communicating cannot meaningfully say 'Amen' to it. '*For you are giving thanks well enough, but the other person is not edified*' (14:17). Paul takes it for granted that what cannot be intelligently shared is unhelpful. '*I thank God I speak in tongues more than you all*' (14:18). It is clear Paul is not against the gift of tongues. The Holy Spirit leads Paul to pray in tongues more frequently than he does in the lives of the Corinthians – a remarkable claim when you remember how much the Corinthians loved the gift of tongues. His words suggest one prays in tongues when one experiences an anointing to do so – otherwise Paul's remark makes no sense. It also tells us that tongues is mainly a private matter since Paul's praying in tongues is apparently not done 'in church'. 'In church' he does something different. '*However in church I wish to speak five words with my mind, that I might instruct others, rather than ten thousand words in a tongue*' (14:19). Paul often writes in a very condensed manner but he is spending a lot of space on this point. He is very eager that the meetings should have nothing in them that people cannot understand. He wants his Corinthians friends to be lively and energetic, but what sounds to the other person like nonsense is not specially valuable in Christian meetings.

Chapter 23

Maturity in Public Worship
(1 Corinthians 14:20–25)

There are four things at least that Paul is looking for from the Corinthians.

1. **He wants maturity in understanding**. *'Brothers and sisters, do not be children in your thinking. On the contrary, be childlike in malice but in understanding be mature'* (14:20). The Corinthians' love of noise and wildness in their meetings is childish. They must learn to value comprehensible revelations from God. They are to be childlike in their love of each other, but, says Paul, let them be thoughtful and mature people. There is nothing wrong with the use of the mind. They must not think that mind-less wildness in the meeting is a sign of advanced maturity in the Holy Spirit!

2. **He does not want tongues to become a judgement rather than a blessing**. He says, *'In the law it has been written, "By other tongues and by the lips of foreigners, I will speak to this people, and not even then will they hear me, says the Lord"* (14:21). *The result is: tongues is a sign not for believing people but for the unbelievers, and prophecy is not for unbelievers but for those who believe'* (14:22).

These verses are emphasized by those who dislike tongues altogether! 'Tongues,' they say, 'was just a miraculous sign of judgement upon unbelievers, so we should not want a sign of judgement to be used in the congregation!' But everything Paul has said so far has been quite positive and appreciative towards the gift of tongues. Paul prays in tongues more than anyone and is quite happy for them to pray in tongues. His only complaint is the wild and unrestrained way they have used tongues in the public meeting. It is impossible to

interpret 14:21–22 in an **entirely** negative manner, as if
tongues were a curse not a blessing.

In Isaiah 28:11–12 (which Paul is quoting), the prophet says
that if the Israelites will not listen to intelligible prophecies,
God will speak to them in an unintelligible manner. God will
send foreign invaders upon the land. The Israelites will be
forced to listen to the unintelligible chatter of the Assyrians or
(later) the Babylonians. The unintelligible talk will be a sign to
them of God's judgement.

Paul's point seems to be – if we follow the context carefully
– that in the way in which the Corinthians are using the gift
they are turning tongues (which ought to be a means of
blessing) into a means of judgement towards outsiders. They
are turning a gift to God's people (tongues rightly used) into
something resembling God's judgement upon unbelieving
Israelites. They are giving a sign to non-Christian visitors
which is entirely wrong and drives them away. Tongues
wrongly used becomes comparable to the unintelligible talk
the Israelites were forced to hear when invaded by the
Assyrians. Paul is not being negative about the gift of tongues,
but he is being negative about the gift of tongues as the
Corinthians are misusing it in public worship. Verse 22 is a
result clause. I translate it: 'The result is . . .'. Paul is dealing
with the result of the Corinthians' poor and immature use of
the gift of tongues.

Paul goes on: ' . . . *and prophecy is not for unbelievers but for
those who believe* (14:22). The first word here is ' . . . and', not
' . . . but' (Greek *de* is here best translated 'and'; it is not Greek
alla which would indicate a strong contrast). Paul goes on:
'and (in the way in which you are doing things) you don't let
unbelievers hear prophecy.' They hear tongues but they are
not present for prophecy – but (says Paul) this is entirely the
wrong way round!

That this interpretation is right is confirmed by the way
Paul continues: '*If therefore the whole church comes together in
one place and everyone is speaking in tongues, and then a person
who does not understand these things comes in or some
unbelievers come in, will they not say that you are mad?*
(14:23). *But if all are prophesying and some unbelieving or*

83

uninstructed person comes in, he is convicted by all, he is judged by all (14:24), *the hidden things of his heart become obvious and so falling on his face he will worship God, declaring that God is really among you'* (14:25).

We note the word 'therefore'. 'If *therefore* (in the way in which you have been using the gift) . . .'. It is clear that Paul is speaking of the **results** that will follow if they continue to act as they have been doing so far.

3. **Paul wants to avoid misunderstanding by seekers or unbelievers**. 'A person who does not understand' and 'some unbelievers' are the same people, but perhaps the first phrase refers to someone who is sympathetic and the second term refers to someone who is more critical. Such people will entirely misunderstand the gift of tongues in the way that the Corinthians are using it.

4. **Paul wants to encourage a situation where unbelievers are likely to be aware of the presence of God**. It is prophecy that will have this effect. *'But if all are prophesying and some unbelieving or uninstructed person comes in, he is convicted by all, he is judged by all* (14:24), *the hidden things of his heart become obvious and so falling on his face he will worship God, declaring that God is really among you'* (14:25). It will often happen that an outsider will visit the church and a word of prophecy will convict him or her in a most dramatic way.

I have told the story elsewhere of an occasion when I was preaching through 1 Corinthians in Nairobi Baptist Church and had got to 1 Corinthians 6:7. The title of the sermon had been announced in the church bulletin: 'Why Not Be Defrauded?' It so happened that there was a woman who had (she said) been defrauded out of some property by someone who attended Nairobi Baptist Church. She came to church that morning determined to have a fight with the lady concerned! She was not interested in the worship but came late to church. She walked in as I announced my text: 'Why Not Be Defrauded?' She told me about it later. 'I came to church furiously angry, but as I walked through the door you were looking directly at me, and you said to me, "Why not be defrauded?" I could not understand how you knew why I had come! I sat down, stunned, to listen to the preaching!'

Sometimes it is even more dramatic. The person might collapse on the ground in distress. Such experiences certainly make us aware that God is present.

After I wrote about that incident,[1] to my surprise yet another man came to me, when I was a visiting preacher back in my old pulpit at Nairobi Baptist Church. He said to me, 'I remember something that happened to me when you were preaching on 1 Corinthians, twenty years ago...', and he went on to tell me of almost exactly the same thing happening to him on the same occasion in the same service! I asked him, 'So what happened in the end?' He said to me: 'I went to a bar where I knew I would find my enemy after church (!) and told him what had happened to me. I told him that I was no longer bothered about the dispute that was between us.'

It sometimes happens that way with prophecy – or with preaching that becomes prophetic – but it does not happen that way with uninterpreted tongues.

Note

[1] See Eaton, *Applying God's Law* (Paternoster, 1999), pp. 00.

Chapter 24

The Corinthian Church Meeting

(1 Corinthians 14:26–33)

Paul is now coming to some conclusions about the help he has given throughout this chapter.

First, he puts to them **what the overall picture should be of worship at Corinth**. He asks: *'What then is the position, brothers and sisters?'* And he gives his answer. *'When you come together, each one of you has a psalm, a teaching, a revelation, a tongue, an interpretation. Let all things take place for edification'* (14:26). 'Each one' should be participating. Several different kinds of ministry should be taking place. Someone leads in singing a psalm. Another person gives some teaching. Another one speaks of something that has been revealed to him which he gives as a prophecy, containing 'revelation'.

These verses are not an 'order of service'! Obviously the entire time is left fairly free. The description is not intended to be complete. There is no mention of any leader! Presumably the church has some elders but they are not so prominent that they have to be specially mentioned. The Holy Spirit is the leader. Paul himself is a lesser leader, giving instructions in these sentences. Some elders would be present but their leadership would, it seems, be even less conspicuous.

Next Paul gives some **principles concerning the gift of tongues** which, as we have seen, was of special interest to the Christians at Corinth. *'If anyone speaks in a tongue, let there be only two or at most three, and let it be one at a time. And let someone interpret* (14:27). *But if there is no one to interpret let the speaker be silent in church and let him speak to himself and to God'* (14:28). Tongues must not dominate the entire meeting. Only two or three may pray in this non-rational way and then only on the understanding that they or someone else has the gift of putting into words what the prayer means. Otherwise the tongues-speakers must hold themselves back, and keep their gift to themselves for the moment. They must not be interrupting each other. The gifts must be exercised one at a time.

Next Paul gives some **principles concerning the gift of prophecy**. *'And let two or three prophets speak, and let the others discern'* (14:29). Two or three prophetic messages should be enough. (The statement that 'all may prophesy' in verse 30 does not have to mean that all may prophesy at every meeting! It simply means that a prophetic word could be given to anyone.) 'The others' – the people as a whole helped by their leaders – should not automatically accept everything that is said. Each prophecy should be considered. Is it in harmony with what is known of God's Word? Is it indeed the voice of the Holy Spirit? Does it truly build up the gathering? Is it needlessly flattering? Is it needlessly cruel and judgemental? Let the others judge. 'The others' does not mean 'the other prophets'. The whole congregation takes part (with a reservation about to be mentioned in 14:33b–35). *'And if something is revealed to another person sitting there, let the first be silent'* (14:30). If another person has a revelation the first prophetic speaker is not to go on so long that the second person is unable to contribute. *'For you are all able to prophesy, one at a time, in order that all may learn and all may be encouraged'* (14:31). The picture is of people helping each other to understand God's will for their lives. All may contribute at one time or another, men and women. The total congregation is involved in helping each other to grow in the things of God. 'When you come together' (verse 26) does not exclude the possibility that some may speak at a later gathering. I doubt whether Paul meant everyone could speak at every meeting!

'And the spirits of prophets are subject to prophets' (14:32). This seems to mean that prophetic speakers are in control of themselves. No one is allowed to say, 'I had to say what I said. I had to go on for that amount of time. The Holy Spirit

compelled me!' No! Everything in 14:27–32 implies that although people cannot give themselves a prophetic message they can control what is happening. An individual is able to stop when another person wishes to speak. You cannot specially bring the Holy Spirit down upon yourself but when God is working powerfully you are still able to control yourself. You are not forced to do anything. The Holy Spirit is not doing anything violent to you.

Then **Paul gives a final word**. He explains something that is at the bottom of everything he has said. *'For God is not the God of confusion but of peace'* (14:33). True worship, true up-building in Christian meetings, is not chaotic. It is not wild and out of control. There is a kind of freedom when the Holy Spirit is at work, yet it is orderly freedom. There is a sense of direction. Unexpected things may happen, but even the unexpected workings of the Holy Spirit do not bring confusion or chaos. The Corinthians were much blessed by the gifts of the Spirit. Paul said that right at the beginning of his letter (see 1:5), but there needs to be a sense of order in their meetings and a few principles that will prevent selfishness, chaos, jealousy, from damaging their worship and their learning together.

What of today? We have to realize that there is more than one kind of Christian meeting. Some might involve an apostle or teacher preaching for several hours (as in Acts 19:9 and elsewhere). But there has to be room for these 'Corinthian' meetings as well, where all are able to prophesy, one at a time, in order that all may learn and all may be encouraged. It is not the only type of Christian meeting but it is one of them and we need them.

Chapter 25

Decently and in Order

(1 Corinthians 14:34–40)

Paul has three more things to say. One concerns the women of the fellowship (14:33b–35). One concerns the willingness of the Corinthians to submit to Paul (14:36–38). And then Paul reaches a conclusion (14:39–40).

1. **The women of the fellowship** (14:33b–35). Paul says, *'As in all the churches of the saints* (14:33b), *let the women be silent in the churches...'* (14:34). What does Paul mean by these instructions? Four guidelines may be followed.

The command cannot be absolute and all-inclusive for there is plenty of evidence that women were allowed to speak in Christian meetings (even in 1 Corinthians – see 11:2–16).

The text is authentic. Although there are some variations in the Greek manuscripts of the New Testament and these verses have been viewed with suspicion, yet there is no good reason for thinking that these words are inauthentic. They appear in all known Greek New Testament manuscripts that have 1 Corinthians (although some manuscripts alter their position). It is not likely that an accidental addition should appear in every known manuscript of 1 Corinthians.

Evasive interpretations should be avoided. The idea that Paul is only saying that the women were too noisy or too uneducated or too heretical is not enough to explain this passage. (Paul refers to all women in all the churches! Note v. 33b.) Surely this passage must be taken in a straightforward manner that fits what Paul has just been saying and does not contradict what we know from 11:2–16.

Verses 39–40 shows that **Paul is still dealing with the theme**

of prophecies and how they are handled. This is surely the key to verses 33b–34. I interpret it as follows.

Paul has an instruction which applies everywhere. *'As in all the churches of the saints . . .* (14:33b). Then he says, *'. . . let the women be silent in the churches. For it is not permitted for them to speak. On the contrary let them be submissive, as also the law says'* (14:34). Paul's point is surely that **the women are asked not to exercise any authority over which prophecies are accepted and which are to be questioned**. It is in this context that they are asked to be subordinate. 'The law' that Paul mentions does not mean the Mosaic legislation. It means 'the Old Testament' (as in 14:21 where he referred to Isaiah). He is thinking of Genesis 2:18–25 (on which he has already commented in 11:8–9). Man was created first. Then the woman was created to be a helpmate for him. It was in that order, not the other way around. In the matter of authority the woman's authority over creation involves her own being under the authority of male leadership. Paul has already dealt with this earlier in his letter.

'But if there is anything they wish to learn let them ask their own husbands at home. For it a shameful thing for a woman to speak in church' (14:35). It is likely that this was a special problem in Corinth. Corinthian women were apparently getting over-excited about taking on leadership in the meetings and being equal with men in every respect. But neither Paul nor the churches will accept their ambitions to break out of the order of God's creation. In Christ they have equal status as Christians and abundant opportunities for ministry, but let women be women and men be men. In the matter of judging prophecy, let the women not seek to be in a position of aggressive authority, says Paul.

2. **The willingness of the Corinthians to submit to Paul** (14:36–38). I do not think verses 36–38 are only attached to verses 33b–35. More likely (since he is drawing this section to a close) Paul is looking back over everything he has said in 12:1–14:35. The Corinthians are behaving in a wild manner. The church is full of rivalries and jealousies. But let them submit to Paul. *'Or did the Word of God go forth from you, or did it only come to you?* (14:36). *If anyone thinks that he is a*

prophet or a spiritual person, let him know clearly that the things I write to you that it is a command of the Lord (14:37). *And if anyone does not know this, let him not be recognized'* (14:38). Submission to apostolic authority is essential. Any truly spiritual person will recognize that Paul is no ordinary person. He is a literal eye-witness of the resurrection, a 'master builder' among the churches. To deny apostolic authority, especially in the case of a first-generation apostle, is to resist God. Anyone who resists apostolic authority (which in Paul's case means New Testament authority) has no status in the churches.

3. **Paul reaches a conclusion** (14:39–40). *'So, my brothers and sisters, be eager to prophesy and do not forbid to speak in tongues'* (14:39). The gift of tongues is all right. All Christians should know something of this kind of non-rational praying. A few Christians will use it even in church meetings, but only on the understanding that it will be turned into something comprehensible. Certainly it must not be forbidden. It is mainly a private gift, but it can become more public and useful when it is not allowed to become chaotic, when it is subordinated to the more important gifts of God-given comprehensible prophecy.

The greatest of the gifts is to speak to others on behalf of God with God-given words. This is what they must seek more than any other gift. We must not make bigger claims than are justified or pretend to have a gift that we do not have. We cannot induce or produce in ourselves any gift. But we can ask God to give us more than we have at the moment. He is likely to give us the desires of our heart if we commit our way to Him, *'... and let all things take place decently and in order'* (14:40).

Chapter 26

Christ's Resurrection

(1 Corinthians 15:1–11)

Paul moves suddenly to deal with a new topic altogether: the
resurrection of the body. Many of the Corinthians' problems
had something to do with the fact that they thought of
themselves as **already** super-saints, already risen with Christ,
so as to be beyond earthly problems. They seem not to have
expected any resurrection further than the **spiritual** resurrection they already had in Christ. Paul has been dealing with
their problems, one at a time, but now he comes to the great
mistake that was beneath many of their difficulties. There is
an even greater resurrection than they have realized, a literal
physical resurrection of the body. They had been taught this,
but it seems they were doubting it. They did not doubt
Christ's resurrection, but they thought that they themselves
were not to expect any greater resurrection than what they
already had. Paul sets out to show them their mistake.

He begins by establishing that they believe in Christ's
resurrection (15:1–11). Then it is illogical of them to doubt
their **own** resurrection. What happened to Jesus will (he says)
happen to them.

Paul writes, *'Now I make known to you, brothers and sisters,
the gospel which I preached to you, which also you received, in
which you stand (15:1), through which you are being saved if
you hold fast to the particular word in which I preached good
news to you – unless you believed in futility (15:2). For I
delivered to you as of first importance that which I also received,
that Christ died for our sins according to the Scriptures (15:3),
and that he was buried and that he was raised on the third day
according to the Scriptures'* (15:4).

1. **The gospel is based on certain facts**. Paul is speaking of events that have happened. His message is 'good news', an announcement of what God has done. It is not simply that men and women are searching to find the right religion or have adopted some religious ideas. God has done something in the history of the world.

2. **Salvation involves receiving what God has done**. You received these things, says Paul. You stand in them. You hold them fast. This is what it means to be a Christian. It means to receive the death and resurrection of Christ as God's way of salvation.

Paul tells us what these basic facts are: 'Christ died for our sins ... He was buried ... He was raised...'. There is no gospel without these basic things that God has done for us.

3. **God's salvation is part of a lengthy programme**. What God did was the fulfilment of what He announced centuries before Jesus came. When Jesus died and rose again it was 'according to the Scriptures', according to a long announced plan that God had revealed.

4. **The resurrection of Christ was witnessed quite literally by many people**. There were eye-witnesses of the resurrection. Paul mentions some of them: '...*and that he was seen by Cephas, and then by the twelve* (15:5). *Then he was seen by over five hundred brothers at one time, of whom the majority are still alive even now, but some have fallen asleep in death* (15:6). *Then he was seen by James, then by all the apostles'* (15:7). There were many literal eye-witnesses of the risen Lord Jesus Christ.

5. **Paul himself was a witness of the resurrection**. We remember the story of how Paul came to salvation. He was a persecutor of the church but dramatically met with the risen Lord Jesus Christ on the way to Damascus. '*And last of all, as if to someone abnormally born, he was seen by me also* (15:8). *For I am the least of the apostles, who am not worthy to be called an apostle because I persecuted the church of God* (15:9). *But by the grace of God I am what I am, and God's grace towards me was not futile, but I laboured more abundantly than them all* (15:10), *but it was not I but the grace of God that was with me* (15:10). *Whether then it was I or they, so we preached and so you believed'* (15:11).

Paul often had to explain his apostleship. God chose him to do a very special work. He was an apostle just like the earlier apostles such as Peter and James and John. But he had a very special ministry. It was his special calling to preach the message of the gospel to gentiles. He had to explain how the Jewish gospel was designed for gentiles. This made him somewhat different. He was like 'someone abnormally born' and was often criticized because of his understanding of how the gospel related to gentiles. In fact he was not in any way inferior to the earlier apostles. But all the apostles preached the resurrection of Jesus, and the Corinthians had believed in the risen Lord Jesus Christ and their lives had been changed.

Paul says all this because he is preparing the way for persuading them that they must believe in the resurrection of **Christians** from the dead. If they believe in the resurrection of Jesus (and they do!), then they already believe in resurrection. Now they must realize that what they believe about Jesus they must believe about themselves.

This is what the gospel is. We receive salvation in Jesus. We are given His righteousness. We are given His status in the eyes of God the Father. We are given His Holy Spirit. We are given His heavenly home. Every blessing comes to us in Christ. When we have Jesus we have everything. The same principle applies to the resurrection. When we have Jesus we shall share in His resurrection. It begins now. We have the power of His resurrection within us immediately. But there is more to come. One day we shall share Christ's resurrection even physically.

Chapter 27

Christ is Risen!

(1 Corinthians 15:12–20)

'*But if it is preached that Christ is raised from the dead, how can some among you say that there is no resurrection of the dead?*' (15:12). Some of the Christians in Corinthians had difficulty believing in the resurrection of men and women from the dead, yet they did believe in the resurrection of Christ from the dead. But this is illogical. If they have believed the preaching that Christ is raised from the dead, how can they deny their own resurrection? No doubt the Corinthians believed in life after death, but they were having problems with believing in the physical resurrection of all men and women. Yet it has serious consequences to deny the resurrection. '*And if there is no resurrection of the dead, then Christ is not risen* (15:13). The two resurrections – Christ's and ours – are linked. It is quite impossible for a Christian to deny Christ's resurrection. So it is impossible to deny our own resurrection also. Paul points to the consequences that follow if the resurrection of Christ is denied.

1. **If Christ's resurrection is denied faith is futile**. Paul says, '*And if there is no resurrection of the dead, then Christ is not risen* (15:13), *and if Christ is not raised then our preaching is futile, and your faith is futile* (15:14), *and we are also found to be false witnesses for God, because we testified about God that He raised up Christ – whom He did not raise up if indeed the dead are not raised*' (15:15).

The entire gospel revolves around the preaching of a physically risen Lord Jesus Christ. If there is no resurrection, then Christ cannot have been raised and everything that the Corinthians have believed through the apostolic preaching must be false because at the very heart of it was the preaching of the resurrection. If Christ's resurrection is denied the gospel is a lie, because it asserts very firmly that Jesus was literally raised from the dead.

The fact is, there is no Christian faith without the resurrection of Jesus from the dead. There can be no half-and-half Christian gospel. We cannot get rid of resurrection and still try to have some kind of Christian faith. True Christians have put their faith in a physically risen Saviour. Their entire faith is misguided if there is no resurrection. Paul is not willing to allow the possibility of a so-called Christian faith without resurrection-faith. Such a 'gospel' would be a weird and grotesque lie.

2. **If Christ's resurrection is denied sin has no atonement**. The Corinthians cannot deny resurrection and yet believe in a risen Saviour. *'For if the dead are not raised, then Christ is not raised* (15:16), *and if Christ is not raised your faith is useless, you are still in your sins'* (15:17). Christ's resurrection was the sign that His sacrifice for our sins is accepted by God the Father. If Jesus died but did not rise again it would mean that Christ died – and that was the end of the matter. We would have no reason to think that there was anything special about the death of Jesus. But in fact Christ's death was not the end. God accepted the death of Jesus as the sacrifice for our sins, and then (having accepted the sacrifice) raised Him from the dead and gave Him all authority to be our Saviour and the King in God's kingdom. If this had not happened our faith would be useless, the sacrifice of Jesus would be without the assurance that God had accepted it. Christians – and everyone else – would be 'still in ... sins'. The guilt and power of sin would still be reigning over us. But actually Christ is raised from the dead! The guilt and power of sin is finished. Sin is not reigning over us. We have died to sin, because Jesus is alive and we are alive with His resurrection-power.

3. **If Christ's resurrection is denied there is no hope for the future**. Our hope of our own defeat of death is linked to our trust in Christ's resurrection. *'And it follows also that those who have fallen asleep in Christ have perished* (15:18). *If in this life only we are people who have put their hope in Christ we are*

of all people the most miserable' (15:19). To think that the Christian life is mainly for this world (as some people seem to think) is seriously to pervert the gospel message. Actually life in this world is tougher for the Christian than for others. In the world we have tribulation. If the Christian gospel is mainly about this life then it is not very successful because the true Christian does not have a specially easy life. If it is only or mainly for this life that we expect to get blessings from God, then we are people to be pitied, for there is nothing specially easy or comfortable about being a true Christian. People who think that the gospel is mainly about health and wealth have not read their Bibles properly. The Christian gospel is mainly about life after resurrection! Life in this world is a matter of preparing for the resurrection-glory that is yet to come. If there is no resurrection, says Paul, it means that those Christians who have died have perished without ever knowing physical and bodily glory. A gospel without the resurrection is pathetic and miserable! *'But in fact Christ has been raised from the dead, the firstfruits of those who have died'* (15:20). There would be no gospel if this were not true, but in fact Jesus is alive literally and physically. And we are getting ready to be physically and literally raised with Him. It is then that we shall enter into the great goal and purpose of salvation: eternal glory with our Lord Jesus Christ.

Chapter 28

The Death of Death

(1 Corinthians 15:20–28)

'*But in fact Christ has been raised from the dead, the firstfruits of those who have died*' (15:20).

1. **Christ the firstfruits**. In the Mosaic law (see Exodus 23:19a; 34:26a) the 'firstfruits' were the first portion of the harvest which was to be given to God when the crops were first gathered. There was a very strong emphasis in the law that there should be no delay in the giving of the firstfruits. They were to be given right at the beginning of the harvest-time. Paul's illustration makes two points. (i) The firstfruits is the sign that the rest is to come. The resurrection of Jesus is the foretaste of the resurrection of all believers. What happened to Him will happen to us. And (ii) the rest of the crop is **later** than the firstfruits. Jesus is raised already. Our resurrection has not yet happened but is guaranteed in due course.

2. **Christ the Last Adam**. Paul goes on to explain how it is that Christ's resurrection guarantees our resurrection. '*For since through a man death came into being, so through a man there will come resurrection of the dead*' (15:21). The procedure that was followed at the time when men and women fell is the same procedure that is followed in the Lord Jesus Christ. Adam was the head of the human race. He was the representative and agent for the entire human race. His very name means 'man'. What happened to Adam happens to 'man'. All humankind was 'in' Adam (see Romans 5:12–21). The entire human race was involved when Adam sinned.

God's way of salvation works similarly. In Christ we are restored. Just as Adam represented us, so Christ represented

us. Christ lived a godly life for us. Christ bore our sins for us.
Christ was physically raised for us. Just as Adam represented
us and brought sin and death into the world, so Jesus
represented us and paid the price for the resurrection of every
member of the human race. Paul goes on: *'For as in Adam
all die, so in Christ all will be brought to life'* (15:22). This is
often read as if it said, 'So all who are in Christ will be
brought to life' – but this is not what it says. It is not referring
to the salvation of the saved: it is referring to the resurrection
of the entire human race. The context is dealing with
resurrection not justification. The resurrection provides **justification** only for believers; it provides **resurrection** for all
people, some to vindication and some to condemnation. 'In'
expresses agency (as in 1 Corinthians 12:13, we note in 15:21,
22 the appearance of *dia* and *en* side by side). By the price-
paying of the Lord Jesus Christ, God raises the entire human
race.

This does not mean that every person is saved, but it does
mean that every person is raised from the dead. Paul taught
that the wicked will be raised as well as the righteous (as we
know most clearly from Acts 24:15; see also Daniel 12:2; John
5:29). Even the resurrection of the wicked depends on the
price-paying resurrection of the Lord Jesus Christ. It is that
thought which Paul has in mind here.

3. **The order of events**. Paul's 'firsfruits' illustration emphasizes that one resurrection is the sign that more resurrection is
coming. *'But each one will be made alive in his own order:
Christ the firstfruits, then the people who belong to Christ will
be made alive at His coming* (15:23). *Then comes the end,
when . . . '*. At this point Paul seems to be arranging his
thoughts in a 'chiastic' manner (an A-B-C-D-C-B-A shape).
The first part (A-B-C-D) focuses on Psalm 110:1; the second
part (D-C-B-A) has in mind Psalm 8:6.

*'. . . **when** he hands over the kingdom to God the Father,
when he destroys all rule and every authority and
power* (15:24).

> *For he must reign until he puts all enemies beneath
> his feet* (15:25).

>> *The last enemy to be destroyed is death* (15:26).

> **For** *"God has subjected all things under his feet".*
> *And **when** he says "All things have been subjected",*
> *clearly God – the one who subjected all things to him –*
> *is excepted* (15:27).
> *And **when** all things are subjected to him He himself –*
> *the Son – will be subjected to God who subjected all*
> *things, in order that God may be all in all'* (15:28).

It is not Paul's purpose to speak in detail about everything that happens at this point of history. His theme is the resurrection. He is not giving an entire survey of everything that could be said. But he says enough for us to know that a lot is to happen! The items mentioned here (which deserve a book in themselves) are (i) 'the end' (events **after** the resurrection of the saved), (ii) the destruction of all that is wicked and evil and in opposition to God, (iii) more specifically, the abolition of death and evil, so that there is no death and no evil remaining in the universe, (iv) the completion of the work of Christ as the mediator between God and man, such that God is all in all.

4. **The final consummation**. Jesus will never finish His work as the Saviour until the saved are raised and death is abolished. Paul says little about the wicked. There is just a hint (in 15:22) that they too will be raised (but without honour, subject to perishability, without immortality). There is a hint here that they will be punished, but it is not Paul's main interest. Then Paul states clearly that ultimately there will be no evil of any kind remaining. All of this will take time. The words 'firstfruits ... then ... then' suggest a period between the Second Coming of Jesus and the final state, in which a lot is to take place. It will be a long period.

Christ too was **under** God as the Mediator, as the God-man. The time will come when Christ's work will be finished. I do not think that Christ will ever cease to be a man. Nor will He ever cease to be worshipped as the one who redeemed us. But there will come a time when His work as the Mediator will be fully accomplished. Christ's mission will have been achieved. Death itself will die! God will have no more enemies remaining. Sin will be powerfully, dreadfully, and lengthily punished. In such a day of resurrection and glory, God's triumph will be shared by His people. We shall be raised in glory. The universe will be raised in glory with us. God will be what He should be in every way in every part of the universe. Father, Son and Holy Spirit will continue their activities forever in a fully peaceful and harmonized cosmos. It is all guaranteed by the resurrection of Jesus, and that resurrection has already taken place. He is the firstfruits; the rest is on its way.

Chapter 29

Arguing for Resurrection
(1 Corinthians 15:29–34)

1 Corinthians 15:28 left us with a breathtaking vision of the
glory that God intends for the universe, and for His people,
but now Paul must return to the task of persuading the
Corinthians that it is all true. He must help them recapture
their hope of their own resurrection to physical glory. First he
puts to them some arguments in favour of resurrection
(15:29–34). He has three ways of urging them to return
to clear resurrection-faith. And then in 15:35 he will begin to
answer some of their questions.

1. **Baptism for the dead**. This is an obscure verse and no one
is completely sure what it means. Paul says, *'If these things are
not true, what shall the people do who were baptized on behalf
of the dead? If the dead are not raised at all, why are people
baptized for them?'* (15:29). One of two possible interpretations seems most likely.

One interpretation takes the verse to mean that some
people had come to salvation but had not had opportunity
to be baptized before they died. So others got baptized 'for the
benefit of' the Christians who had died. Perhaps they felt
nervous (unnecessarily) about a Christian dying unbaptized.
Paul's use of the word 'those' or 'the people' (not 'you')
suggests that only a few were doing this. Paul has already told
the Corinthians that being baptised is not a magical protection. It seems that the Corinthians specially valued the
symbols of baptism and the Lord's Supper. They felt they
had some kind of protection coming from these two signs and
symbols. Paul has already rebuked this (10:1–2), so does not
need to do so again. Now he simply points out that it is

strange to practise this sort of weird baptism for dead people – but not believe in the resurrection. If this is a correct interpretation it must be remembered it was only a peculiar practice of some Corinthians and Paul does not approve of it. Getting baptized in the hope that it will somehow benefit dead people is an idea found nowhere else in the New Testament or in Christian history.

There is another interpretation which might be right. Sometimes a person would become a Christian and live for Jesus. Then the Christian would die – perhaps even dying for his or her faith in Christ. People who watched him or her would be so impressed that they would come to faith in Christ and would express their faith in baptism. They would be baptized for the sake of – out of regard for – what they had seen happen in the life of their friend who had died. Paul's point is: what would be the point of that if a Christian is never raised from the dead?

Either way, Paul is arguing that the Corinthians' custom implies a hope in final resurrection.

2. **Compensation for suffering**. He continues: *'Why are we ourselves in danger every hour?'* (15:30). Paul and his fellow-workers lived a very difficult life. But what is the point of this way of living if there is no resurrection and it is all for this life only? If Paul and his friends are not to be resurrected and are not to be given reward for what they have suffered, and the Corinthians themselves are never to be raised, then why bother with such a difficult life?

Paul reminds them of the kind of life he lives. *'My brothers and sisters, I die daily!'* Every day he faces the prospect of death from his various enemies. Every day he has to surrender the hope of an easy life. *'I protest, brothers and sisters, by the pride that I have in you which I have in Christ Jesus our Lord'* (15:31). Paul gives a kind of oath. 'I take an oath,' he says, 'by that which is most precious to me – which is you yourselves. I have a kind of "pride" in you. You are my hope of heavenly reward. You and people like you are the people I glory in more than anyone else in the world. I swear by what is most precious in my life, that I have to surrender to the prospect of death every day of my life. So why should we apostles suffer like this if there is no compensation for our sufferings – in resurrection-reward?' *'If I fought with "beasts" at Ephesus, struggling merely on a human level, what have I gained?'* (15:32a). Paul is speaking metaphorically. When he was living and preaching in Ephesus it was like being a trained fighter, fighting with animals in a circus. Paul teaches that resurrection is the occasion of heavenly reward. If there is no resurrection-reward, what is the point of all of his struggles?

3. **A stimulus to godliness** (15:33b–34). *'If the dead are not raised, let us eat and drink, for tomorrow we die'* (15:32b). Resurrection-reward is the motivation for the godly life. We may as well forget godliness and simply indulge ourselves if there is no resurrection-reward. But Paul asks his friends to come back to true and clear resurrection-faith. *'Do not be deceived. Bad companionships corrupt good behaviour'* (15:33). There will be a damaging effect in their lives if they keep listening to those who do not believe in resurrection-reward. *'Sober up and come back to your right mind. Stop sinning. For there are some people who are ignorant of God – I say this to your shame'* (15:34). Resurrection-reward is the stimulus to the godly life. Their present style of faith and life is a delusion. Its theology is wrong. Its impact upon their lives will be disastrous. They must forget about being 'super-saints' who can sin as much as they like because the body is shameful and only the Holy Spirit matters! Let them resist the temptations of the flesh, and let them start living for resurrection-reward.

Chapter 30

Questions About Resurrection

(1 Corinthians 15:35–44)

Paul now turns to answering questions that might be asked about resurrection. First, he puts **the questions**. *'But someone will say, "How are the dead raised?"'* It is a staggering and amazing thing to believe that anything good can come from a corpse. Nothing tests whether we believe in the miraculous more than whether we believe in resurrection. *'"With what sort of body do they come?"'* (15:35).

Then, he gives **a rebuke**. Paul says: *'You are being foolish!'* (15:36a). (Cultures vary in how they take statements like this. 'You silly thing' is a friendly, amused statement in some cultures – but a great insult in others. Paul's phrase was not very insulting but it was a word of mild rebuke. Luke 24:25 is similar. I try to translate it accordingly.)

Next, there is **an illustration**. Paul uses a picture taken from planting seeds. *'The thing that you sow does not come to life unless it dies* (15:36b). *And the thing that you sow is not the body which is about to come into being, but a bare grain maybe of wheat or of some other grain* (15:37). *But God gives it a body, just as He wished, and to each of the seeds He gives its own body'* (15:38). When you put a seed into the ground it is like a burial. To all appearances (and Paul is using the language of appearance) it is dead and buried, never to be seen again. Planting a seed is rather like a funeral!

But actually something amazing happens to that seed. A few months later that seed will blossom into something that looks entirely different from the dry dead-looking thing that was planted. This is the way it is with resurrection. You bury a dead body. Who could dream that the person would ever be seen again in a physical body? But he will be! Paul's Corinthian friends who are doubting resurrection are in fact being foolish. They are imagining they can philosophize their way to the truth. But the Christian gospel is not a matter of philosophy or logic. It is a matter of revelation from God. We can use our minds, but we need God's revelation as a foundation for all our thinking. Our bodies will one day be cremated or put into the ground. But it is just planting a seed. Something entirely different will appear, somehow arising from that dead body.

The next point is: **the resurrection body is radically new**. We must not make the mistake of thinking that resurrection is resuscitation. The final resurrection will **not** be like Lazarus' coming out of the grave (when the same old Lazarus was brought back to the situation he was in before). Resurrection is **not** a corpse having life breathed into it. When you plant a seed and a plant arises from it, the plant is very different from the seed. How does a seed turn into a bougainvillea plant, a banana tree, a tulip? It is a radical and surprising turn of events when something arises which is so different in appearance from what was sown.

Next: bodies have great variety. *'Not all flesh is the same flesh, but there is one kind of flesh for human beings, and another kind of flesh for animals, another for birds, and another for fish* (15:39). There is very great variety in the bodies that we know on earth. Human bodies have two legs to walk with, an amazing brain to think with. Most animals walk on all fours. Fishes have gills to allow them to live in water. Birds have bodies which are extraordinarily light in weight. What variety there is! Paul's point is: we can expect the resurrection body to be very appropriate to the glory that we are approaching.

Then he goes a stage further. *'And there are heavenly bodies and earthly bodies, but the glory of the heavenly bodies is one thing, and the glory of the earthly bodies is something else* (15:40). *There is one glory for the sun and another glory for the moon and yet another glory for the stars. For one star differs from another star in glory* (15:41). *This is the way it is in the resurrection of the dead'* (15:42a). Again, there is variety in the heavenly bodies. The sun gives light and warmth and energy. The moon shines dimly. The planets wander over the sky. The stars are only dots of light which stay on course more than the planets. Again: what variety! There is variation in glory: some shine more brightly than others.

This all illustrates the resurrection. Our resurrection bodies will be appropriate to the heavenly realm. An important point to notice is that there is variation in glory. Some shine more brightly than others. Paul seems to have this aspect of the matter on his mind because the theme of reward constantly surfaces in this letter (notably in 1 Corinthians 3:9b–15; 9:23–27) and in this chapter ('What shall I gain?' v. 32). Verse 58 will use this very point. It is not a waste of time to work hard because it is rewarded in the resurrection. One star differs from another star in glory (15:41). This is the way it is in the resurrection of the dead (15:42a). Christians will be 'like the stars for ever and ever' to the extent that they have turned many to righteousness – as Daniel 12:3 puts it. There will be stunning change and great variety in the last resurrection, including variety of brightness. The level of holiness we have reached will be visible forever.

Finally, we have a **description**. Paul lets us know something of what the resurrection body will be like. *'It is sown in corruption; it is raised in incorruption* (15:42b). *It is sown in dishonour; it is raised in glory. It is sown in weakness; it is raised in power* (15:43). *It is sown a natural body; it is raised a Spiritual body'* (15:44a). The resurrection body will never deteriorate (but the bodies of the lost will be without the imperishability). The resurrection body will have glory – the visible outshining of holiness, greater in some than in others. The resurrection body will have power. We shall have greater strength, heightened faculties. The resurrection body will have the Holy Spirit in a greater way than ever. There are three levels in the working of the Holy Spirit:[1] in bringing people to new birth, in the 'sealing' and 'anointing' of those who have believed, and in the final resurrection where our 'Spiritual bodies' (capital 'S' referring to the Holy Spirit) will be greater channels of the Spirit's power than ever before.

Note

[1] See further, Eaton, *1, 2, 3 John* (Christian Focus, 1996), pp. 77–78; G. Smeaton, *The Doctrine of the Holy Spirit* (Banner of Truth, 1974 reprint), pp. 122–149.

Chapter 31

Two Adams

(1 Corinthians 15:44b–49)

Paul now develops the thought that the resurrection-body is not simply a resuscitation of our old corpse. It will be something radically different.

Two kinds of body. *'If there is a natural body, there is also a Spiritual body'* (15:44b). The word 'natural' is the same word that was used in 1 Corinthians 2:14. The Greek is *psuchike* – 'a soul-ish body', 'a body characterized by having ordinary human life'. All people are body-and-soul. They have body and human personality joined together in tight unity.

This is the nature of all human beings. We may translate it 'a natural body', a body which is the vehicle of ordinary human energy. But there is also a 'Spiritual body', a body which is perfectly filled with the glory given to it by the Holy Spirit. ('Spiritual' does not mean non-material; and it does not mean 'adapted' to the higher human nature, the 'spirit' (small 's'); the word always relates to the Holy Spirit.)

Two Adams. The two bodies relate to Adam and Christ. *'So it is written, "The first man Adam became a living person. The last Adam became a life-giving Spirit"'* (15:45). We can be certain of our resurrection because of our relationship to the Lord Jesus Christ.

The 'Adam' of Genesis 1–3 was a historical person. God created a first man. Paul refers to Genesis 2:7b, but does not quote it with exact precision. The Hebrew uses 'the man' and does not have the word 'first'. 'The first man Adam became a living person' (Greek: *psuche*); he had a natural (*psuchikos*) body, a body designed for ordinary life in this world, a body adapted to being a person (*psuche*) in this world. When God created Adam He 'breathed into His face the breath of life'. Adam was a body; he became a living body (a 'person') by the breath of God breathing into the dust.

But – says Paul – 'The last Adam became a life-giving Spirit'. This is an extraordinary statement. It echoes the language of Genesis 2:7a which led to Genesis 2:7b. Just as God had life-giving power, so now Jesus has life-giving power as the risen and glorified Lord Jesus Christ. It is this life-giving divinely powerful person who will bring all of His people to be risen as He is risen. It is difficult to translate the term 'Spirit' here. It does not mean that Jesus became the Holy Spirit. It has the idea of 'powerful life-giving person'. The first Adam was life-**receiving**. Adam could only give people his **natural** likeness (remember Genesis 5:3; the human race could only reproduce 'naturally'). But the last Adam is life-**giving**. Christ gives His people His own spiritual likeness – including His resurrection body. We can only get to the highest form of living in the Holy Spirit by resurrection, and only Christ can bring us there. And that is what He will do for all His people. The unsaved will be raised to condemnation but Jesus raises His people to the highest form of living in the Holy Spirit – by giving them bodies filled with the power of the Holy Spirit.

The chronological order of the two bodies. *'But it is not the Spiritual body which is first, but the natural body and afterward comes the Spiritual body'* (15:46). We know of one kind of human nature, but God has always had plans to take us into a higher kind of human nature. We were born with one kind of body, but God has always had plans to take us into a higher phase of existence with a higher kind of human body. It will be given to us as a reward. Paul has to say this because the Corinthians seem to think they have the higher kind of body already (see 4:8). Paul says, 'No. You are still in the first stage. The resurrection body comes later!'

The nature of the two Adams. *'The first man was out of the earth earthy, the second man is out of heaven'* (15:47). Adam was made from the dust of the earth. He was weak and vulnerable and open to the possibility of falling into sin. The second man has a new resurrection-nature. Jesus has powers He did not have before. When raised from the dead He said,

'All authority **has been given** to me.' This is what Paul is referring to here. He is not speaking of Jesus' first origin from heaven as a man in His first coming to earth. Rather he is speaking of the heavenly origin of His human nature **now**. The Lord Jesus Christ **now** has a human nature that does not come from the dust but is directly given to Him by God. Our bodies will be conformed to His body (see Philippians 3:20).

Two humanities. Paul says, *'Such as is the earthy person, so also are the earthly ones; and such as is the heavenly Man, so also are the heavenly ones'* (15:48). The old humanity inherited their bodies and their fallen nature from Adam. The new humanity, Jesus' people, will inherit new bodies with a new glorified human nature – from the Lord Jesus Christ.

Two images. *'And as we have borne the image of the earthly man, we bear also the image of the heavenly man'* (15:49). Sin and death and judgement came into the world because we came in the 'image' of Adam, carrying his sinful nature, with his spoiled, ruined, weak, natural body. But for those who live for the Lord Jesus Christ we are now taken out of Adam, and we are in the image of Christ, who is Himself the image of God. It has started already; we are already being transformed into His likeness. But there is a stage still to come. We shall be in 'the image of the 'heavenly man', Jesus, even in our very bodies.

Chapter 32

The Great Victory

(1 Corinthians 15:50–58)

A great change is coming and a great victory.

1. **We are looking forward to a great change**. In
1 Corinthians 15:50 Paul picks up a sentence from verse 47
('The second man is out of heaven') and explains it further.
*'Now I am saying this, brothers and sisters: it is not flesh and
blood that can inherit the kingdom of God, and corruption does
not inherit incorruption.'* Paul's point is not that the resurrection body is not physical, but that the resurrection body
does not arise out of the powers and capacities of the
body that we have at present. Our natural body does not
have the ability within itself to rise from the dead.

Invariably in the New Testament 'inherit' refers to reward.
Paul uses the word 'inherit' because resurrection is part of and
is the occasion of heavenly reward. Paul has already referred
several times to 'gaining' reward (3:12–17; 9:15b–18) and he
warns us that lack of love will lead to us losing our reward
(13:3), and that without resurrection there is no reward
(15:32a). Now he uses the idea of 'inheriting' to make the
same point. There is variation in glory: some will shine more
brightly than others (15:41b). Our hard work is not in vain
because it will be rewarded in resurrection. What happens in
resurrection is the beginning of our inheritance.

Resurrection is not within the present resources of our
body. It is a miracle. *'Behold, I tell you a mystery. We shall not
all fall asleep, but we shall all be changed* (15:51), *in a moment,
at the glance of an eye, in the time of the last trumpet'* (15:52a).
Some Christians will not die at all. But all Christians will
receive a glorified body. The resurrection body does not

112

evolve out of our present body; it comes dramatically. In the time of the Israelites in the wilderness the trumpet sounded when the people of God were about to move on to the next stage in their travels. The resurrection will be the greatest change, the greatest forward move there ever was! *'For the trumpet will sound and the dead will be raised incorruptible and we shall be changed* (15:52). *For this corruptible body must put on incorruption and this mortal thing must put on immortality'* (15:53). In one way or another (whether we die or not before the event) all Christians will 'put on' a new, glorified body. We are raised to death-less-ness. Before, we were perishable but now we shall be deathless. The Bible never speaks of the sinner being immortal. The wicked are raised to face 'long-protracted torment with raging fire',[1] but are still perishable and will experience 'the second death'. The godly **put on** immortal, incorruptible, glorified bodies.

2. **We are expecting a great victory**. *'And whenever this that is corruptible shall put on incorruption and this that is mortal shall put on immortality, then the saying that was written shall come to pass. "Death is swallowed up in victory."* (15:54)

"O death, where is you victory?

O death, where is your sting?"' (15:55)

Hosea had a long-term vision of the day when death would be abolished. He had been thinking of death and destruction coming upon Israel (Hosea 10:14), and of the time when God lifted up His voice against Israel and Israel died (Hosea 13:1). He has referred to the death-dealing self-destruction of idolatry in which Israel is exterminated. Now he turns to the exact opposite: the day when the last enemy, death, will itself be destroyed. 'I will ransom them from the power of Sheol; I will redeem them from death'. Hosea is envisaging the resurrection of Israel. We might ask: was Hosea thinking of individual resurrection from the grave? It is hard to see how any kind of limit can be put on Hosea's prediction. Any thinking person would surely have to ask the question: but is sin and Sheol **completely** defeated or is it defeated only within this life? Since the 'wages of sin' include physical death as well as a damaged relationship to God, Hosea's talk about deliverance from Sheol must mean deliverance from physical death as well as from a damaged relationship with God. So Paul had clear vision when he applied Hosea's words to the resurrection. And he could add a bit more and tell us what the thorns and the sting actually are. *'The sting of death is sin, and the power of sin is the law* (15:56). *But thanks be to God who gives us the victory through our Lord Jesus Christ!'* (15:57).

There would be no fear of death if it were not for sin. The reason why death is the king of terrors is because we face it with sin in our record and sin on our conscience. Only for the one who is in Christ is the sting removed. The law does not make things better; it makes things worse. The more we seek to fulfil the tenth commandment, the more the law stirs up sin in our fleshy appetites. Victory comes from elsewhere altogether. Jesus gives victory over condemnation, victory over law, victory over the wages of sin which is death.

Paul's last word here is: *'Therefore, my beloved brothers and sisters, be firm, unmovable, always abounding in the work of the Lord, knowing that your labour is not in vain in the Lord'* (15:58). This again proves there is variety in the level of glory we receive in our resurrection body. How could there be a 'therefore' and talk about the 'work of the Lord' if all Christians were equal in resurrection? We are to abound in the work of the Lord because one star differs from another star in glory. Abundant labours lead to abundant reward – in resurrection glory. Christians look forward to the day when their bodies will be transformed and glorified. Our reward will be made visible in our bodies! Soon we shall be in a glorified world with glorified bodies, with the words of Jesus echoing around the universe: 'Well done!'

Note

[1] Arnobius, *Adversus Gentes*, books 2, 14.

Chapter 33

Concerning the Collection

(1 Corinthians 16:1–4)

Paul moves from the most profound topic in 1 Corinthians, the resurrection, to the most practical matter. *'Now concerning the collection ...'* He has just mentioned our 'labour in the Lord' (15:58). Now he comes to one of those labours: financial support.

1. **Paul has a great concern for the unity of the churches**. His concern to help the churches of Jerusalem financially went back to the early days of his ministry. At least as early as AD 47 when he paid his second visit to Jerusalem (Acts 11:30; Galatians 2:1–10) Paul was concerned to help the needy Christians of Jerusalem and Judea. He obviously continued to be concerned about the financial needs of Jerusalem, because now, a few years later, we again find him raising financial support for the Christians at Jerusalem. In 1 Corinthians 16:1–4 we discover that he wants the church at Corinth to set aside funds for this work of assisting Jerusalem. The Corinthians would (in conjunction with other churches, I suppose) send representatives to Jerusalem when the gift was complete. *'Now concerning the collection for the saints: as I gave instruction to the churches of Galatia, so also you must do the same'* (16:1).

The next mention of the matter will be in 2 Corinthians 8 and 9. When he talks about 'the saints' (2 Corinthians 8:4) and people who are in need (2 Corinthians 8:13–14) he is thinking of the Christians in Jerusalem. He tells the Corinthians that they should be generous and should try to bring about more fair-sharing between the destitute churches of Jerusalem and the Christians in Corinth. Paul will mention this collection again in the letter to the Romans 15:25–29.

The churches of Judea were Jewish; the church in Corinth was very largely gentile. Paul is wanting gentile Christians to support the Christians in Judea who were culturally quite different from themselves. One reason why he was specially concerned about this matter was that the support of the poorer Jewish Christians by the wealthier gentile Christians was a way of making it quite obvious that there was only one church of Jesus Christ. Paul was very concerned about the unity of the churches. Not only did he want the churches of Corinth and Galatia to be doing something similar, he also wanted his churches in Corinth and Galatia to express their unity with the churches in and around Jerusalem. Churches are not to exist in isolation from one another.

2. **Paul has a concern for practical matters**. One might think that an apostle's work is purely doctrinal or spiritual, but he takes the trouble to give advice over very practical matters. *'On the first day of the week let each one of you put aside something at your meeting, storing it up, as each person may prosper, so that when I come special collections need not be made'* (16:2). The Christians evidently met on the first day of the week. It was not a 'sabbath' for them, but it was something they chose to do. They had to choose at least one day to meet and they avoided the day on which Jewish people worshipped. Sunday was a good choice. It is not a law but it has now become an established Christian tradition. In places where it is inconvenient there is no special law about it and another day might be chosen if necessary.

The phrase which I translate 'at your meeting' generally means 'at home' but the reference is obviously to the meeting of the congregation. They are to put something aside each week into some kind of church treasury. Paul wants steady regular giving, not panicky special offerings at the last moment.

3. **Paul has a concern to co-operate with the people**. It is interesting to notice how the helpers who must travel to Jerusalem are to be chosen. *'And whenever I arrive I will send whichever people you approve with letters of commendation;*

they will take your gift to Jerusalem' (16:3). The people will do the choosing. Paul will do the appointing. We notice the similarity to Acts 6:3. There is great wisdom in doing things this way. The people will know whether any person ought not to be chosen because he has some special weakness. (Perhaps he is never around except when the apostle visits Corinth!) The apostle might not know the Corinthian people as well as they know each other. Yet the people do not do the appointing. The apostle does that (and therefore has the possibility of vetoing a choice if he is not convinced). We can learn much about the appointment of church officers from this example. The apostle and the people each have a part to play in this matter.

4. **Paul has a concern for continued involvement with what the people are doing**. He cannot leave it entirely to them. He must continue to watch over what is happening, keeping himself informed. And he may be needed to take part in the travelling himself. *'And if it is advisable for me to go also, then they will go with me'* (16:4). We remember that when he travelled with a gift to Jerusalem once before (Acts 11:30), it was an opportunity for him also to discuss matters with the leaders of Jerusalem (I assume that Galatians 2:1–10 refers to the same occasion). It is likely that Paul thought that once again it might be useful to combine two matters at the same time. If so he is willing to travel to Jerusalem with the offering that the churches have taken up. Romans 15:25–29 lets us know that this plan was in fact taken up by the apostle and he did travel with the funds to Jerusalem. He was still keeping involved with what all his churches were doing and maintaining their unity with the churches in Judea.

It all goes to show what practical matters are involved in Christian ministry.

Chapter 34

Plans and Opportunities
(1 Corinthians 16:5–12)

These closing words of Paul may seem unimportant and yet they provide us with a useful glimpse of some of the lesser-known aspects of his work. We see his plans, the opposition he faced, and his work of supervising his churches in a loving and gracious manner.

1. **His plans**. He shares with the Corinthians what he hopes he will do. He is writing from Ephesus, and says, *'And I shall come to you when I shall have passed through Macedonia. For I am travelling through Macedonia* (16:5), *and perhaps I shall stay with you or even spend the winter with you, in order that you may help me on my way, wherever I may go'* (16:6; compare Romans 15:24).

Paul was writing 1 Corinthians from Ephesus, in Roman Asia Minor. His plan was to travel around the coast through Asia Minor, Thrace and Macedonia until he reached Corinth. He would be able to visit Philippi and Thessalonica on the way, where he had churches that he had founded. Eventually he hoped to reach Corinth and spend time with them.

We notice that Paul is making his plans provisionally. He says, '**perhaps** I shall stay with you'; he is not certain. God's guidance leaves room for us to make some plans of our own. We do not always live by special and detailed guidance. God leaves us a certain amount of freedom, and uses our own desires and our own intelligence.

Actually Paul did not do precisely as he planned and this caused him some difficulty with the Corinthians later on (as we learn a couple of pages further on in our New Testaments, in 2 Corinthians 1:15–17).

'For I do not wish to see you now just briefly in passing; for I am hoping to remain with you for some time, if the Lord permits it (16:7). *But I shall remain at Ephesus until Pentecost* (16:8), *for there is open for me a large and very promising door, and there are many enemies'* (16:9). Paul's words here let us know what it was that gave him guidance and a knowledge of God's will – at least provisionally. He was influenced by opportunities that came for him to serve God, and work that had to be done. He says '**and** there are many enemies' not '**but** there are many enemies'. What he means is: he feels he has to stay to help the Ephesian Christians. But however much he may have his own plans, he knows that God may overrule. 'I am hoping ... if the Lord permits it,' he says. He knows God may plan otherwise – and in the event Paul did not do quite as he had planned.

2. **His adversaries**. 'And there are many enemies,' says Paul. No forward work of the gospel comes without arousing the opposition of men and women, and behind the opposition of men and women is the opposition of Satan. Any Christian worker or evangelist must expect it and prepare for such hindrances, from people, from circumstances, from one's own weaknesses. There will always be many hindrances, yet if we persist in faith we shall overcome them.

3. **His work in supervising the churches**. He has words of advice for a variety of circumstances. *'Now if Timothy comes, see to it that he is with you without any fear, for he is doing the work of the Lord just as I am* (16:10). *Let no one despise him. Help him on his way in peace, in order that he may come to me, for I am awaiting him with the other brothers and sisters'*

(16:11). Timothy needed a word of support from Paul. He was a timid person, it seems, though he must have been very gifted for Paul to work with him so much and so closely. The Corinthians were difficult people to work with at times, so Paul specially asks that they will be helpful to Timothy. It is all part of his practical handling of men and women in the churches, some of whom might be difficult!

'And concerning brother Apollos, I earnestly pleaded with him to come to you with the other brothers, but it was not at all his will that he should come just now. However he will come when he has the opportunity' (16:12). Paul keeps the Corinthians well informed about what his plans are, as best as he can. For some reason Apollos was not eager to visit Corinth just yet.

The picture here is an interesting one. We know little about the church officials in Corinth. Verses 15–17 refers to some of them, so it would be a mistake to think that there were no leaders in Corinth (although they are not prominent in 1 Corinthians 12–14). In addition to local leaders there were travelling workers of different kinds who worked with Paul. From what Paul says about Apollos they did not issue them with over-authoritarian instructions. Their own wishes were taken into consideration. But clearly we have here a large team of workers with different groups travelling all over the Mediterranean world, and with Paul seeking to hold them all together and make good use of them.

It is apparent also that Paul did not feel threatened by other gifted workers. Apollos is known to have been a gifted teacher of the gospel. It is quite likely that he was more gifted speaker than Paul and he is very likely to have had greater literary knowledge than Paul (since he came from Alexandria which had the largest library in the ancient world and was famous for its books). Yet this does not trouble Paul. He is a leader of the work, but feels well able to share it with a whole team of workers and assistants, some of them very gifted people.

All this is typical of Christian work. We shall have to be men and women with plans. We shall certainly have enemies. And we need friends and colleagues.

Chapter 35

A Fivefold Appeal
(1 Corinthians 16:13–14)

Paul is getting close to the end of his great letter. Now he fires off a string of five sharp commands: *'Be on the alert. Stand firm in the faith. Be people of courage. Be strong* (16:13). *Let all that you do be done in love'* (16:14). These are his concluding exhortations. We recall the problems the Corinthians had: their divisiveness, their wildness and instability, their moral problems, their tendencies to get involved with idolatry, the aggressiveness of the women, the misuse of the Lord's Supper, their extremism in the use of the gifts of the Spirit and – above all – their thinking there was no physical resurrection because they had been raised bodily already! Paul does not give up on them. He does not doubt their conversion. He does not bring them under the Mosaic law. He has been appealing to them in a Christian manner not a Mosaic manner.

1. **Be on the alert**. The trouble with the Corinthians is that they have been careless in watching for mistakes in their lives. We all tend to take things for granted. We think we are sufficiently experienced and are not likely to make any big mistakes. Then Satan comes at us from some unexpected angle. There were things happening in Corinth that ought never to have happened. They had slipped into all sorts of mistakes because of lack of watchfulness. Paul says: Be on the alert. Be watchful. Don't be sleepy and careless.

2. **Stand firm in faith**. It is not so much 'the faith' that Paul has in mind; that gives the impression of something purely doctrinal. By 'the faith' Paul means 'the habit of trusting God no matter what happens'. There are all sorts of difficulties and troubles facing the Corinthians but they must go on believing.

121

This is the secret of the Christian life: it is to go on believing no matter what happens to you. Discouragements, delays, oppositions, weaknesses, tragedies, the most unexpected disasters. God has purposes and plans in everything that happens to you. Let nothing discourage you. When you make mistakes, get up and keep going. There are times in life when we think that life is finished – but the story has not ended until it has ended. Stand firm in faith. Go on believing no matter what. Jonah thought life was finished for him when he was in the fish's belly – but his greatest ministry had not yet begun. Moses thought that life was finished for him when he was two-thirds of the way through his life as a shepherd in Midian. But his greatest ministry had not yet begun. Go on believing. Stand firm in faith.

3. **Be people of courage**. The Christian life can be scary at times. We look at the circumstances we are in and the dangers we face of many different kinds, and we say to ourselves, 'Can I survive? Will I be able to keep going? What will happen to me if this takes place – or this, or that? Corinth was a tough place to live in. It was full of paganism and idolatry. Temptations and testings were to be found on every side. Paul says: be people of courage. Don't be faint-hearted. Don't be anxious. Look to God to help you. Don't be cowardly.

4. **Be strong**. The command is not exactly identical to the previous one. The difference is that 'Be people of courage' looks to the future and the things that might intimidate us. But 'Be strong' considers where we are right now. It will require strength to defeat Satan. Where can such strength come from? From the Lord Jesus Christ! The Christian learns to lean on Jesus. We are not to be surprised or afraid at this conflict. We are to stand! Our Lord Jesus is there at our side. He is ready to give us assistance. We have to fight but Jesus is near at hand. Sometimes when the battle is strong He will draw specially close and will say to us, '*I am with you ... no one shall attack you to harm you ...* ' (Acts 18:9–10). Almighty power is at work for us and in us. The secret of victory is to know that the Lord Jesus Christ is strong and yet He is willing to give His strength to us. We see our strength in Jesus. We look at the victories of His life, His miracles, His wisdom, His

conquering Satan and all his friends. And then we recall that same 'might of His strength' is available for us. We are 'in Him'. His strength is ours. We live by the faithfulness of the Son of God.

5. **Let all that you do be done in love**. The Christian life all comes to a climax in the life of love. This is what everything leads to. This is what God was seeking for from the beginning of the history of salvation. He wants to produce a people of love. Not sloppy love! Not lustful love! Not sentiment. Not play-acting condescension. But strong, adult, mature, thoughtful love towards other people. This kind of love keeps the 'Golden Rule' in mind. You do not need a book of rulings about what to say or do in difficult situations. Asking God to lead us in the pathway of loving the other person will lead us in the right direction in a thousand-and-one situations. It leads us into asking the right questions. It is practical. You talk to yourself and ask yourself a few questions. How would I like to be treated if I were where that person is. Then you act in love towards them. You make a habit of it. You do it all the time. Let all that you do be done in love.

Chapter 36

Grace and Love
(1 Corinthians 16:15–24)

At times one feels like asking the question: are there no leaders in Corinth? Paul does not seem to say much about elders and deacons! Did they not have much part to play in Corinth? Probably the answer to this is that there were church 'officials' but the Corinthians were much more interested in gifts than they were in officials. But Paul does not handle problems about gifts by pointing to the officials of the church! What he wants to do is get the gifts functioning properly! Yet, at this point it is likely that Paul is asking for respect for one of the leaders of the church.

1. **He asks for respect for the leadership in Corinth**. Paul's first converts were often the people who became leaders in the church. In any pioneer situation this tends to be what happens. Now he has a word to say about one particular family, and other leaders in Corinth. *'Now brothers and sisters, I urge you. You know the household of Stephanas, and how they were the firstfruits of Achaia and they devoted themselves to serving God's holy people'* (16:15). Stephanus is clearly a leader in the church who had been loyal to Paul. *'I urge you to submit yourselves to such people and to everyone working with me and labouring at what they are doing'* (16:16). So there are Christian leaders in Corinth after all! One could hardly have guessed it when we were reading chapters 12–14. Paul has put gifts above officials, but there are some appointed officials in Corinth and now Paul mentions that he wants them to be followed and obeyed. They are people who have experience; they were among Paul's first converts.

Paul has been missing contact with the Corinthians. He says, *'And I am rejoicing at the arrival of Stephanas and Fortunatus and Achaicus, because they have supplied what you were not able to give me* (16:17), *for they refreshed my spirit as they have refreshed yours. Give recognition to these people'* (16:18). It seems some of the leaders had travelled to Ephesus to tell Paul what was happening. It helped Paul a lot. He was blessed by their sharing with him what was happening and their discussing and no doubt praying over the needs of the Corinthian Christians. Paul found it refreshing. What the people of Corinth had not been able to do, some of their leaders have been able to provide for him.

2. **Paul sends his final greetings**. Paul seems to regard these greetings as very important. They come in every letter he ever wrote. *'The churches of Roman Asia greet you. Aquilla and Prisca greet you, and so do the church that is in their house* (16:19). *All the brothers and sisters send greetings. Greet one another with a holy kiss'* (16:20). It might be thought that these greetings are simply unimportant formal courtesies and do not require much attention from us. Yet greetings are more important than we might think. When little courtesies are omitted a lot of ill-will and suspicion are created. No church will stay together for long without them. No apostle can afford to neglect them. A 'hello', a 'good morning' or a 'farewell' or a 'Praise God' are little points-of-contact in friendship. They do not seem very important and yet when they are lacking their absence is disastrous and will damage relationships. Any person wishing to maintain friendship will take care of the little greetings!

Paul regards this matter as so important that at this point he takes the pen from his secretary or scribe and writes a greeting himself. *'The greeting of Paul comes to you – in his own handwriting'* (16:21).

Paul wants to hold the church together in love and harmony. Yet at the same time he is quite severe about not recognizing anyone who refuses to submit to the revelation of the gospel in the Lord Jesus Christ. In a few words Paul sums up his feelings about them. *'If anyone does not love the Lord, let him or her be "anathema" – under God's curse'* (16:22). The most important thing is that he and all of his friends in Corinth submit lovingly to the Lord Jesus Christ. Anyone who is unhappy about that is not a Christian at all and will come eventually under God's judgement. Paul's curse on such a person is not an expression of hate. It is simply a realistic statement that salvation is only to be found in our Lord Jesus Christ. Anyone who has no relationship to Jesus is not a Christian at all and has no business being identified with the Christians of Corinth. *'Our Lord come!'* says Paul (16:22). At an early stage of his letter (1:7–8) he had described them as a people eagerly waiting for Jesus to come. This is what it means to be a Christian. We do everything under the umbrella of a soon-to-take-place coming of Jesus, about which we are very eager. If Jesus does not literally and finally and physically come soon, He has other ways of coming. He can end a situation very abruptly! He can come in judgement. He can come in sudden revival. In one way or another the coming of Jesus is always near.

His final concerns are above grace and love. *'The grace of the Lord Jesus be with you* (16:23). *My love be with you all in Christ Jesus'* (16:24). This is how the church of Jesus survives. There were many problems in Corinth but Paul is optimistic about them. God's grace is still available. Paul still loves them. When you have a gracious God and an inspired apostle writing a New Testament document for you (whether he knows it or not) you have all that you need for life and godliness.

Some Further Reading

G. Fee's *1 Corinthians* (Eerdmans/Paternoster) has made most other commentaries to be somewhat redundant. He replaces the older expositions (with obvious titles) by Bruce, Barrett, Robertson and Plummer. Yet Fee is tough reading, and does not do more than make basic suggestions about applying the message to the churches, and I am sorry he rejects the authenticity of 1 Corinthians 14:33b–35. Calvin and Charles Hodge are always worth reading. At a simpler level I am not sure what to recommend. There does not seem to be an entire work on 1 Corinthians which is more advanced than this one, but simpler than Fee. Some major series of commentaries being produced at present have not yet got to 1 Corinthians and so we await those which will appear in the Word Commentary series. Kistemaker comes nearest to something lengthy but easier than Fee, but is not totally satisfying in chapters 12 and 14 of 1 Corinthians. We shall have to wait for something better, which is thorough but recommendable to the ordinary pastor. Meanwhile this 72,000-word offering of mine in two books will have to fill the gap for some people.

On particular sections of 1 Corinthians good work has been done by W. Grudem (*The Gift of Prophecy...*; various editions); J.B. Hurley (*Man and Woman in Biblical Perspective*, IVP); D. Carson (*The Cross and Christian Ministry*, IVP; *Showing the Spirit*, Baker); M. Turner (*The Holy Spirit and Spiritual Gifts*, Paternoster), and others. Jonathan Edwards on 1 Corinthians (*Charity and its Fruits*) is perhaps the greatest work he ever wrote.